Creating the

Writing
Portfolio

Alan C. Purves
Joseph A. Quattrini
Christine I. Sullivan

NTC *Publishing Group*
Lincolnwood, Illinois USA

The preparation for this book occurred while the three authors were working on a portfolio research project supported by the Educational Research and Development Programs as administered by the Office of Educational Research and Improvement, United States Department of Education, Grant R-117G10015. The material and opinions presented in this volume are the sole responsibility of the authors and were prepared independently of the research project.

Executive Editor: John T. Nolan
Project Manager: Marisa L. L'Heureux
Cover design: Ophelia M. Chambliss
Interior design: Ellen Pettengell
Production Manager: Rosemary Dolinski

CONTENTS

2
Getting Started   26

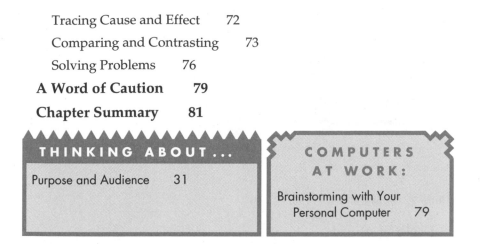

3

Giving Shape to Your Writing 82

5
Writing about Literature   150

6
Revision   178

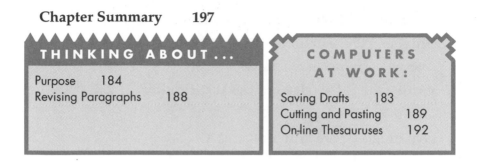

THINKING ABOUT...

Organizing Your Portfolio for an Audience   224

COMPUTERS AT WORK:

Polishing, Arranging, and Displaying   232

Appendix
A Short Guide to Practical Grammar and Style   **235**

PREFACE

This book is the result of a collaboration among three people who have been working together for two years on a project on the use of portfolios in literature classes. During those two years, we came to see the importance of talking about portfolios with the people who actually have to assemble them: you. Hence this book. It is written to and for you, and it comes out of our firm belief that the best way to help you write well in school is to clarify the rules of the game. It's hard to play a game if only one team knows the rules and if that team hires the referees as well. To many students, that's the way school is, and we do not think it is a necessary state of affairs.

In at least one sense, this is not a traditional composition textbook in that there are not a lot of assignments and exercises. Our assumption is that the best writing comes out of the work you do in class by collaborating on a project or out of the work you do as an individual who feels the need to write.

Our book focuses on the problems you face when you enter a writing class and have to consider creating a portfolio of your work. There are problems involved in planning the portfolio, thinking about writing, getting started writing, creating the first draft, working on a revision that will "speak" to a specific audience, preparing a final draft, and compiling the formal portfolio itself.

We hope the book will be practical and, to some extent, fun. We would like to make the writing classroom an enjoyable place to be, a place where people come together to share their experiments, plans, hopes, and judgments with each other. It should not be a place where you must compete to get grades from an "enemy" instructor, but one where you can learn together. It should be an environment in which you can create a portfolio that best portrays your strengths and potential as a writer and as a student of writing.

Features of This Book

Each chapter begins with a **preview** ("Looking Ahead") and ends with a **summary** so as to help you find what you may be looking for and so that you can be prepared to go into the chapter and find specific advice or pointers.

There are **lists** in this book. Many of them are headed "Thinking About . . ." You should go over the lists and use them as a way of checking what you are doing. Sometimes you will need to answer the question that is posed in some detail and in writing; other times you may need only a checkmark. Treat the lists like many of the other checklists in life, such as those for getting ready to drive a car (Is my seat belt fastened? Is the mirror adjusted? Is the emergency brake disengaged?) Use them until they become a habit. Then you won't need to refer to them because they will have become second nature.

We have included **samples of student writing** to indicate some of the possibilities for responses to assignments or suggestions. These are not necessarily the very best that could be done (although we think most of them are pretty good), but they should suggest ways of dealing with the problem at hand.

There are a number of **writing exercises** to help you keep your "writing muscles" in shape. These are exercises that will help you become relaxed about writing rather than being nervous about it. They will help you get ideas for longer papers and will help you shape your writing so that people will want to read it.

A part of each chapter ("Computers at Work") deals with issues that arise for those of you who are using computers in your writing. We have tried to make these **computer application sections** useful for you, whatever sort of computer you use—whether it is your own or one you have to "borrow" in the computer center.

We have included an **Appendix** that gives useful information about grammar and style. This is not a grammar book, but a book on writing, and we think that your knowledge of grammar should be used to help you write better. The appendix looks at grammar from a functional perspective and explores some of the options you might try.

A Few Words About Writing and Work

Many aspects of school are about what as a student you need to be able to list, identify, classify, label, match, or otherwise show you know. Recently, there has been a strong movement in the U.S. to include in the curriculum more instruction about work. Unless there is a drastic change in the approach to the curriculum, much of the new information will be presented in the form of lists, identifications, classifications, and the like.

What will be missing, we fear, is experience in how to work and how to enjoy it. We hope you will find that this book helps you to learn how to work as a writer and how to enjoy it. We want your experience to include knowledge, but also to focus on practice and habits. What you know is most useful and satisfying when you know how to use it and know enough to use it.

The three of us work as writers. We couldn't if we didn't know how, and we wouldn't if we didn't enjoy it.

Acknowledgments

We would like to acknowledge the support in preparing this book that we have had from all sorts of people. We are particularly grateful to those students who suffered through our trials of various exercises and experiments with portfolios. We are grateful to the other teachers in the portfolio project who shared their ideas with us. We are grateful to Executive Editor John Nolan and Developmental Editor Susan Moss who helped us immeasurably by being there when we needed them and by supporting all of our quirks. Finally, we are grateful to our families, who gave up precious time so that we could finish this.

1 Using Portfolios to Take Control of Your Writing

Do You Know:

- What a portfolio is and what it says about you?
- How to define and negotiate your goals?
- How to use a working portfolio and construct a presentation portfolio?
- How to make a plan to develop your portfolio?

Looking Ahead

This first chapter will explain that a portfolio shows the world the variety of things you know, you can do, and you have done. When you're developing a portfolio, you have many things to manage at the same time. We'll show you how to take control by making a long-range plan to guide yourself through the work.

Because you will need to make a thousand decisions between now and the time you present your portfolio—from cover design to preparing a final grade proposal—you will see how to get started on managing a working portfolio and constructing a final, or presentation, portfolio.

And you'll learn a little of our approach to writing: We ask more questions than we give answers, because we think writing is more about the questions than the answers.

This book is about writing and about how you can take control of your performance as a writer in and out of school and college. Taking control is not easy; it requires work on your part, but then nobody ever said that writing was going to be easy . . . or school and college, or life, for that matter.

The point of this book is simple: that what you write and the way you write is a part of your public self. Of course, some of the writing you will do is only for your private self, but most writing is done for people who cannot see you because they are far away or will look at what you have written at some time after you wrote it and went on your way. Each piece that you write is a public document, whether it is a public of the one person you want to impress (like a rich relative) or a large anonymous group of people to whom you want to report something (like readers of the letters-to-the-editor section of your local paper). This public aspect of writing is particularly important in school and college, where you are not only asked to do things—like write—but also to explain how and why you did what you did.

You cannot be judged as a writer on the basis of one essay or test. Everybody knows this in real life—one sip doesn't make a swallow; never go by first impressions; a single game doesn't make the season. But sometimes people seem to forget it and play up the big test. To judge your writing and to evaluate you as a writer, instructors and administrators need to look at a fair sample of what you have done.

When you write in school and college (and if you think about it, you probably do a lot of writing for all your courses as well as for some of the co-curricular activities you participate in), sometimes you are writing for yourself, sometimes for your instructor, and sometimes for other students. Each time you write, you are writing to be read. And each time a reader reads what you have written, she or he will make a judgment about the quality of what you write, about its clarity and its interest level. You may even judge your own class notes two months after you wrote them and wonder what could have possessed you to have written things so difficult to understand or remember. All readers (and you are no exception) are armed with two weapons: a marvelous capacity to misunderstand what has been written and an amazing urge to lose interest in the subject and the writer.

You have to be prepared, to anticipate, and to counter those two weapons.

Is it fair for a person to judge your writing on the basis of a single piece? We don't think so. A "good" writer, most people agree, is one who is articulate (who can be understood easily), who is fluent (who can write easily and often), and who is flexible (who can do different kinds of writing equally well). That is why we are suggesting to you and your instructors that you make a *portfolio* of your writing.

A Portfolio Approach to Presenting Yourself

This book is about a particular format in which you can present yourself as a writer, the portfolio. A portfolio is a collection of the various things that you have done. A portfolio can be used by other people to judge your quality as a performer or artist, in this case a writer. Portfolios are used by people in all sorts of worlds.

In the professional world, a portfolio is what an artist or a business person takes to a prospective employer or client. It is the first glimpse that many people have of that person. A portfolio is an amplified resumé. It seeks to show the person off to the world, to say, "Here is what I have done; look at it as an indicator of what I can do." It includes things that the person has created or helped to create and it contains comments on or and reviews of those things. Some of the people who carry portfolios include: painters, musicians, hair stylists, dressmakers, dancers, photographers, livestock breeders, actors, architects, landscapers, advertising people, car modifiers, interior decorators, sales persons, writers, rodeo clowns, and chefs.

The common element in the portfolios of this group is a sample of accomplishments. The portfolio may include actual samples like tapes or videos or stills or pieces of writing; it might include testimonials or reviews; it might include letters from people who have been impressed by what has been done; it usually includes some sort of statement by the person about who he (or she) is, where he has been, and where he wants to go.

As these people proceed through their careers, they keep updating their portfolios. They constantly reorganize and redevelop their portfolios with different items for different purposes: to get a job, to enter a competition, to plan a publication. They review the contents to make sure their skills and abilities are still portrayed as they want them to be; they may even write a new introduction to the various parts.

Portfolios in School and College

So far we have discussed portfolios in professional settings; we think this same approach should apply to academic settings, particularly to writing. The writing portfolio is not merely a collection of papers or drafts of papers that you accumulate in a folder or in your English notebook. It is not an internal document for you alone or you and your instructor. It should contain those items which best represent your accomplishments to a broader world; it is your personal statement and testimonial to your skills and interests. Some may be things that have been assigned, while others may have been freely chosen. What you might seek to develop is a way of showing what you know about writing, what sorts of writing you can do for your courses, and what sorts of writing you do on your own. Throughout this book, we will keep returning to these three facets of you as a writer: what you know, what you can do if you are really put to the test, and what you do on your own.

Think of the portfolio as a museum of you, or as your self-portrait. Any museum is arranged for the viewer and any portrait is taken from an angle. And the room in the museum or the angle of the portrait may vary depending on your purpose. We do not know what it is you want to show about yourself, what you want to emphasize; you will need to make these decisions for yourself. One kind of portrait might have an angle of mastery, proving to the world that you are indeed competent. Another angle might exhibit you as a thoughtful, sensitive writer with an artistic flair. A third angle might show how you have grown and changed over a period of time. Still another angle might show you as a member of a community of writers who have mastered a new language such as English and who are no longer seen as having a problem with the language. In most cases, your portfolio also portrays you as a responsible human being.

A portfolio is not like a test, an examination, or a course grade. Its value is hard to summarize in a single number or letter. That is why it exists. A portfolio shows the world the variety of things you know, those you can do, and those you have done. It is designed to show your range (the variety of things you can do) and your depth (the degree of care with which you do them). It should reflect what has been going on in your class and what sorts of tasks and opportunities have been offered to you. Your portfolio should contain a statement of the goals of the course and the school. This way, anyone looking at the portfolio should be able to reconstruct the writing program that you have had, should be able to identify the program's objectives, and should understand what the criteria and standards of accomplishment are. The portfolio may also include a list of writing related opportunities provided such as the business education course, print shop, student paper or magazine, or the various writing contests and awards that are available.

Needless to say, your portfolio should be created by you. It may contain the guidelines from the school or the instructor about the kinds of things that might (or must) be included, such as a number of kinds of writing, a self-evaluation, a list of books read, or a number of original compositions or performances in media such as film or music. It may have some pieces you worked on as part of a team. But decisions as to what specific pieces should be included and how they should be arranged should remain yours. After all, it's your writing and your reputation that are on the line.

The Working and Presentation Portfolios

You will probably have two versions of the portfolio—a *working portfolio* and a *presentation portfolio*. The working portfolio is what you are in the process of forming for the duration of your writing course. It is like the draft of a paper or the series of rehearsals of a play or a concert. There will be rough edges, pieces you may want to change or pitch. It is for you and perhaps one or two other students and your instructor to look at.

Most of this volume will take you through the steps of making the working portfolio, but the last chapters will discuss the presentation portfolio. This is the performance, when you lay it on the line for others to see. You are saying good-bye to your portfolio. You cannot change it or fix it up anymore; you may not even be there to explain it to someone else. It has to stand on its own as a representation of you. It is you to the big outside world, the audience. It is scary to let go, we know; we have had to do it with this book. The book is there for you, we aren't, although we would like you or your instructor to write us or call us and tell us what you think or ask us to clear something up. But we know that the book will have to do most of our talking for us.

So it is with your final portfolio. It's yours, not anybody else's.

Taking Charge by Taking Responsibility

Since the portfolio is yours, you must be responsible for it. Taking responsibility doesn't begin on the last day of the course—it begins on the very first day.

THINKING ABOUT . . .

Taking Responsibility for a Portfolio

Ask yourself:

- What should I include in my portfolio?
- How should I arrange the contents?
- What sort of cover and format should it have?
- Should I revise each piece? How?
- Should all of my writing pieces be uniform? Should I use the same font in my printer? Should I do some things in calligraphy?

- How should I include collaborative or group work in it?
- How should I show my contribution to a large project such as an anthology or a collaborative writing project?

As you answer these questions, you will see that you are laying yourself on the line before the whole class, perhaps, or before a jury of instructors. It is your choice as to whether you should be seen as an apathetic student or as one who takes pride in his or her work. Your instructors cannot make this choice for you. The other students can't help you either. You are on your own.

Getting Started

To get started, you should think of yourself as a writer—an apprentice writer at least. Like mechanics, golfers, or chefs, writers are concerned both with what they produce and with the way they go about producing it. Most writing courses deal with both the process of writing and the various products or compositions. It's like being a chef. You think about various aspects of the dishes you are going to prepare: what they will look like, how they will taste, what order they will be served in. You also think about menu planning: what to buy, what order to prepare various dishes or ingredients, how not to waste energy or utensils, how to make sure everything is ready on time.

In the list of questions about taking responsibility for your portfolio, we mentioned both of these aspects of being a writer. We mentioned what the portfolio might look like and how you might go about putting it together. When you consider any writing assignment, you are probably thinking about what the final product should look like and the process, the best way for you to get to that product. Both of these are important and should be in your mind as you work through the course and develop your portfolio.

THINKING ABOUT . . .

The Product

Ask yourself:

- What should it look like? This refers to the physical appearance. Writing is something produced for the eye; it has a visible shape. (Think about the margins, the typeface, whether you will use pen or pencil, the neatness, the spelling, the grammar, and all sorts of other features that help readers take your marks and turn them into words, sentences, feelings, and thoughts.)

- What should it be about? This is the question of content. Am I going to write about myself or keep myself out of it? Am I going to have a lot of facts and specific bits of information? Am I going to focus on the environment, or on human rights, or on race in my writing?

- How should it be organized? How will my writing be shaped? Where do I want to begin? Where do I want my readers to end up? How will the parts be arranged? What sorts of connections and patterns do I want to make?

- How can it show me as a writer? What tone of voice do I want to use in my writing? Do I want to be seen as a sure person or one who is always considering the options? Do I want to be seen as a poetic type noted for the interesting word or metaphor, or as a person who is simple and straightforward? Do I want to be elegant or plain?

You should also think about the ways you want to appear as a person who writes, as a craftsperson.

THINKING ABOUT . . .

The Process

Ask Yourself:

- How should I handle time? Should I start thinking about the assignment right away, or should I put it aside until I have a long stretch of time to think about it? Should I get it in early?

- What sorts of tools and materials will I need? Do I need the library or some research tools; do I need to use a computer? Do I need to interview or otherwise work with other people?

- How should I work with others? Do my classmates and I get together to plan the writing? Do we work together on the research or the early drafts? Do I do peer review and writer's conferences? How do I work with the instructor? With others inside and outside of school? In all of these collaborative efforts, am I a leader, a helper, or a more passive participant?

- How should I go through the steps of writing? (Many people break these steps down into planning [what goes on before a person actually writes], drafting, revising, and editing to make the final copy.) How should I plan? Should I work on an outline? Should I jot down as many ideas as I can? Should I be satisfied with the first way it comes out? How should I get feedback and best use the opinions of others? How will I decide when it is finished and ready to turn in?

These are questions you must deal with each time you write and each time you consider your portfolio. There are no best answers to any of these questions. Many people with vastly different habits of working and conceptions about what is a good piece of writing are equally successful in the eyes of the outside world.

Setting Goals for Yourself as a Writer

It is important that you set your own goals and make your own plan for what you want to accomplish as a writer and as a student. No one can do it for you. The three questions mentioned earlier are the most important ones to start with.

Goal Setting

Ask yourself:

- What do I want to know about? What sorts of things about writing or the ways in which other writers act and think would I like to learn about? (For example, would you like to know the best way to organize a term paper, or what the tricks of humorous writers might be?)

  In our classes, one student wrote: "I want to know how to write openers that get people to read my papers."

- What do I want to be able to do? What technical skills and abilities would I like to have that I can depend on? (These might be skills like making more effective transitions, using creative metaphors or analogies, or spelling more accurately. Abilities like these might not be things that you use every time you write a letter, but they are often useful.)

  One of our students wrote: "I'd like to learn how to figure out an examination question." Another wrote: "I'd like to learn how to use vivid words in my writing."

- What habits and practices do I want to develop? What sorts of things do I want to become a permanent part of my repertoire as a writer, such as checking what I have written for clarity or making sure I have planned what I write before I plunge in? Do I want to become more serious as a writer? Do I want to work with others more effectively? Do I want to be more independent? Do I want to have more fun? Do I want to write more, and enjoy it more, too? How do I want to handle my writing in other classes?

  A student wrote: "I'd like to learn how to budget my time better." Another wrote: "I'd like to learn how to take criticism better."

  Your answers to these questions will become your learning plan, your set of goals and objectives as a writer. Keep them in the front cover of your working portfolio. Look over your list of goals and think of how you might attain them.

Negotiating Your Goals

How do the goals that you have set fit in with the goals set by your instructor? The two of you may have to negotiate them. In most cases, the two of you can work together. Say that your instructor wants you to be able to write without making so many spelling and grammar errors, and you want to be able to write down the way you see and feel about the world. Are these two goals so different? Ask yourself:

- Why do I want to write down the way I see and feel about the world?
- Who do I want to read my thoughts and feelings?
- What do I want them to understand?
- How can I help them get my drift?

One answer to this set of questions might be that if you want other people to understand how you feel about the world you need to have them get your message. People get the message easily if they don't have to worry about the surface of the message—that is, if the message is easy for them to read. One way of making it easy is to get all the technical problems out of the way. We have tried to make this book easy to read, but if you had to figure out what the words were or where one thought stopped and another started, you would have trouble interpreting our meaning. That's why we checked our spelling and grammar and got an editor at the publishing house to help us.

Finding Out the Criteria for Good Writing

One of the best ways to begin to take charge of your writing in school and to make a successful portfolio is to find out as much as possible about the rules of the game. This is something you should ask your instructor to share with you at the beginning of the course. You need to find out what she or he means by being a good writer.

Many instructors give out their grading standards at the beginning of the course. A grade sheet we have found useful looks like this:

	Poor				*Excellent*
Discourse-Level Qualities					
Quality and Development of Ideas	1	2	3	4	5
Organization and Structure	1	2	3	4	5
Style and Tone	1	2	3	4	5

Text-Level Qualities	Poor			Excellent	
Grammar and Wording	1	2	3	4	5
Spelling and Punctuation	1	2	3	4	5
Handwriting and Neatness	1	2	3	4	5
My personal reaction	1	2	3	4	5

Comments:

We will discuss these sorts of grading sheets in greater detail in Chapter 7. If your instructor does not hand out a detailed explanation of terms like the ones in this list, you should ask her or him to clarify these standards for you.

Beyond grading sheets, for individual papers, you will find that instructors believe that some aspects of being a good writer are as follows:

Handling the Process of Writing. This includes successful completion of planning exercises, revising what you have written with other students acting as a trial audience, reviewing the final copy, handing in the paper on time, and other acts like using paper clips, budgeting time, or reading and following up on feedback that writers develop for getting their work done well.

Dealing with Content. This includes following the kind of research that might be required as well as determining the point of view you are to take toward the subject. You will also need to gauge the amount of room you have to include personal opinion, the degree to which you should take other people's opinions into account, and other aspects of the "what" that goes into your papers.

Dealing with Organization. This includes trying the kinds of openings and closings that are considered effective, determining the amount of detail that is needed, choosing the kinds of signals to connect your ideas, and using other methods to hold the chunks of a piece of writing together.

Dealing with Style. This includes deciding what sort of language is considered appropriate: Should it be full of metaphors and images, or should it be matter-of-fact? What about slang and technical terms?

Dealing with Format. This includes deciding what kind of paper to write on, whether it is to be done on a word processor, how important correct spelling is on this version, where you should put your name, and other aspects of the visual appearance of the document you submit.

Remember that your instructor is an important audience. Not the only audience, but an important one who represents that larger world of readers who will finally judge your portfolio, the various pieces in it, and, by inference, *you* as a writer and as a student. Your instructor is often the coach who is there to help you write your best. Sometimes the instructor is also the judge, the person who determines your success as a writer.

Keeping Process Notes

Another way of taking control and maintaining it, especially as you are planning your portfolio and doing the work during the course, is to keep a set of process notes or a log of your work. This should be a record of what writing you did when, and what your thoughts are while doing the writing. As you finish each paper or writing project, you should assemble those notes into a process memorandum. We discuss this further in Chapter 7. Look at it now, and you will be prepared.

Grouping

Using the technique known as "grouping," an effective form of reflection that has been used in other contexts, is another way of taking charge of your writing. It is different from the collaborative writing (where you and some colleagues work on producing a joint composition) or peer tutoring (where students read each other's writing and provide feedback) that might go on in your class. It is aimed at encouraging you and your peers to consider yourselves as writers so that you can become more active in your work.

As a way of having you think about yourself as a writer, grouping is based on the idea that people do better in reaching their goals if they can *share* the goals—and their ups and downs—in private. Grouping depends upon having the members of the group use the same format each time they meet. The format is usually one of questions about how the members of the group are progressing towards a set of goals that they have defined. The group members share their answers to those questions each time, talk with each other about them, and encourage each other. It is a time of sharing and reflection, generally not one of admonition or assessment (other than self-assessment). What goes on in the group is confidential.

Every two weeks you and your group should get together for a half hour and share answers to the following questions. These questions are based on the questions that formed your plan of learning. Each time the group meets, members should take turns answering each question. It is good to have one person be the leader of each grouping session, but you should rotate leaders. You may have your working portfolio in front of you as you answer each of these questions:

- What do I know that I didn't know?
- What can I do that I couldn't do?
- What do I do that I didn't do?

This is your time for review and reflection. It is different from any conference time you may have with the instructor. You should have the conference time as well, so that you can take the unresolved questions from your group to the instructor, who can help you learn more or do better.

Making a Working Portfolio

We said at the beginning of this chapter that a portfolio is not simply a folder containing all your writing. It isn't a notebook, either—not the one you will be carrying around and doodling in all year. It isn't a drawer in your desk at home or the floor of your locker at school into which you toss everything, nor is it a knapsack or book bag. You will probably have at least one of those means of storing the various pieces you have written over the course of the year: your drafts, notes, revisions, comment slips, and the like. It should be a safe means of storage, and you would probably be better off if you didn't carry it around with you everywhere.

Set aside a place for keeping your writing, one that you can come back to whenever you have a chance to review your final portfolio. (In some courses, the working portfolio is kept in the room in folders or bins provided by the instructor.) This place is your working portfolio, your file from which you will draw the various things that you will eventually put into the final portfolio. How you organize the material depends on you. You might file things by date, by subject, or by some other sorting system. If you keep a lot of drafts of things you are working on but are not a compulsive file maker, you would be well advised to jot a date on each sheet of paper. Doing so will help when you review your work.

Remember that the working portfolio is only the raw material for the portfolio you will share with others and hand in to be judged. It is necessary to the final portfolio, but don't make the fatal error of shoving the whole bag at the instructor and saying, "Here, you make sense of it." That's a sure way of failing.

Putting It All Together

As we mentioned at the beginning of this chapter, your writing portfolio should be a comprehensive picture of you as a writer. A good writer is articulate, fluent, and flexible. A good writer can work independently or as part of a team. This means that when you come to consider the final presentation portfolio at the end of the year, you will be looking over everything you have written to see how it can show each of these aspects of you to your best advantage. But you should begin that thinking early in the course of the semester or the year. We take up some points here that we will return to in Chapter 8, which discusses the final portfolio in some detail.

First, think about how you want to be seen. As we will repeat later, people tend to judge based on first impressions. *It isn't fair, but it's life.* Therefore, one way to start thinking about your writing and your portfolio is to sketch the idea for the cover now. You can always change it, but making the cover will help you think of yourself as a writer. How do you want to be seen? How do you want to say hello to your readers?

Sketching the Cover. The cover is the first impression of you as a writer and of what one will find inside the portfolio. What should it look like? Should it be plain, a blank? Should it just have your name as if that tells all? Should it be illustrated? If it is to be illustrated, what do you want to show people? Images? Words? Photos? Drawings? A collage? Should it be in color or black and white?

Figure 1.1 shows a possible form for a portfolio cover. The cover design, like the works within the portfolio, is a public presentation of you. The cover is the basis for the first impression that readers will get of you as a writer and as a person. It is like a mask that can both hide and reveal your strengths and weaknesses, your hopes and aspirations. We recommend that you sketch a cover design now, show it to other students to get their reactions, and then think about how you might want to revise it.

Second, take stock of your opportunities to write. One way to do this is to take a survey of your various courses and identify your chances to write. After all, not all of your opportunities will come in English courses. In fact, in English class you might not even have a chance to write essay examinations that demand a lot in a short amount of time. You might not have a chance to write up a joint research project that occurs over a lengthy period. You might not have a chance to write an explanation of a mathematics or science solution. You might not have a chance to write a detailed accident report, take lecture notes, or keep the minutes of a meeting.

FIGURE 1.1 POSSIBLE FORM FOR PORTFOLIO COVER.

To help you take stock of all the writing you do, try a checklist or planning sheet like the model in Table 1.1. (In Chapters 3, 4, and 5 we will go into greater detail about some of these kinds of writing.)

Of course, you might want to expand the table by using a separate page for each horizontal row. The idea behind this form is to help you get a sense of how many different kinds of writing you might do in the course of the academic year. These are not really separate categories into which you can neatly put each piece of writing, but they are areas of focus for writing. They show how writing can occur in different settings and serve different functions.

TABLE 1.1 WRITING PORTFOLIO PLANNING SHEET

Purpose for Writing	Assignment Information	Course or Subject	Co-curricular Activity	At Work	On My Own
Writing to Remember (example: notes)	Number Average Length Collaborator? Time Constraint Criteria for Success Select for Portfolio				
Writing to Express Myself (example: a response journal)	Number Average Length Collaborator? Time Constraint Criteria for Success Select for Portfolio				
Writing to Inform Others (example: a lab report)	Number Average Length Collaborator? Time Constraint Criteria for Success Select for Portfolio				
Writing to Convince Others (example: an argument)	Number Average Length Collaborator? Time Constraint Criteria for Success Select for Portfolio				
Writing to Make Something Beautiful (example: a poem)	Number Average Length Collaborator? Time Constraint Criteria for Success Select for Portfolio				

A good way to approach this planning device is to take it from class to class for a week and see what parts of it you can fill out either from actual assignments or from information you get from instructors and other students. You might add to this form during the course of a marking period.

As you fill it out, some of the questions you might ask yourself about each assignment or writing task could include the following:

THINKING ABOUT . . .

Writing Assignments

Ask yourself:

1. How would this task show me as an articulate writer?
    *   What will it tell about my handling of content?
    *   What will it tell about my handling of structure and organization?
    *   What will it say about my handling of the language?

2. How would this task show me as a fluent writer?
    *   How will this task show how I handle time? Will it be done under pressure?
    *   How easy will it be to write this?
    *   How often will I have to write pieces like this?
    *   In how many different courses or situations will I write pieces like this?

3. How would this piece show me as a flexible writer?
    *   How is this different from other tasks in the kinds of demands it places on me as a writer? Do I have to come up with original ideas? Do I have to come up with my own way of organizing it?
    *   How is it different from other tasks in the purpose or function of writing?
    *   How is it different from other tasks in the sort of audience for whom it is intended? Is it for the instructor only? For others in the class? For strangers? For myself?

4. How would this task show me as an independent person or a team member?
    *   Will I work entirely on my own? If so, how will this show in the way I worked on this piece of writing?
    *   Will I work with others? If so, what role am I to play? How does my influence show? Am I supported by the others, or do I support them?

As you examine each task in this way, you will be developing a profile of the sorts of writing you will do and the sort of writer you are practicing to be during the year. Look over the planning sheet and questions at the end of the year when you work on assembling your final portfolio. We will come back to it and help you work through portfolio assembly in Chapter 8.

Selecting Material Written Outside the English Course

Your review of your writing will mean that you will have to go into that working portfolio you have been avoiding looking at for so long. It's like cleaning out your locker at the end of the year. The working portfolio probably has most of the writing you have done in English courses. And we will be writing about that quite a bit. But you have probably also been writing in other subjects as well.

For example, translation from a foreign language could show your control of both languages; a case study from a psychology course could show your ability to relate your academic learning to personal experience and human behavior. A solution you developed in a technology course— a drawing, recipe or procedure, marketing analysis, or advertising brochure—might be accompanied by a process memo that shows how you went about planning, drafting, revising, and finishing a piece of work. We will discuss this writing in greater detail in Chapter 4, but below are a few things to consider as you review what you did in those courses to determine what might be in the portfolio.

Social Studies Writing. In a social studies or history course, you have probably written answers to quizzes and examinations and you might have done a long paper as well. More likely than not, this was a paper that involved some form of research. It might have meant going to the library and reading in books, journals, and newspapers. It might have been a project in which you interviewed people and wrote up the results. The examination questions might have been like the following:

List the major causes of the French Revolution and discuss the probable importance of each.

To do well on this type of examination question, you would have had to read your textbook or the other assigned sources, be able to extract a list of causes from the paragraphs you read, and remember them. You also need to have thought about those causes or followed the discussion of them in the reading or in class, to determine what the criteria for "importance" are, and then to apply them to the list you have generated. If this was an in-class examination, you would have had to remember the information along with a lot of information for other possible questions. In a take-home examination, you would have had the chance to review your notes.

Write a paper of five pages in which you trace the effects of the American Revolution on the people living in northern New Jersey from 1776 to 1781. Using your textbook and the sources listed in the bibliography, show how the "average" family was affected by the British and Revolutionary soldiers and by the economic and political forces of the war.

To succeed in this kind of assignment, you need to explore the source that you have been given, take reading notes related to the topic of the paper, prepare a citation list for the bibliography, find a thesis you can support with the evidence you have, and outline and draft the paper. All of this will take time and it will show that you are able to use sources, establish and prove a point, and present the paper in the academic form (footnotes and bibliography) that is required. (We will discuss this kind of paper in some detail in Chapter 4.)

Both of these examples probably are somewhat different from the sort of writing you have done in English courses. In the examination, you are probably expected to give as much factual information as you can in a short amount of time. This is a writing skill that you might want to demonstrate in your portfolio.

The research paper is also one you might want to include, as it requires you to gather evidence to support a thesis. When such a paper is evaluated, the emphasis is often on the quality of the evidence. Ask yourself:

- Are there enough examples?

- Do they all lead to the same conclusion?

- How did I handle conflicting opinions about the same topic?

- How well did I document my conclusions?

- Is the bibliography extensive?

Science and Mathematics Writing. The kind of writing you are asked to do for science and math courses is usually restricted to factual description. In both subjects, the facts—the observations, tests, and proofs that you set down on paper—are what matter. The purpose of your writing is (a) to let the facts speak for themselves as much as possible, and (b) to describe your procedure so clearly that anyone else can repeat (the technical term is *replicate*) your procedures and thus test your conclusion. It's just like writing a recipe for a cookbook. You are trying to convince others with the evidence, not with your skill as an arguer. Look at the following example.

In an Earth Science class (with a partner) you are to take a series of repeated readings of the temperature in Celsius of the earth and the atmosphere at ground level and six feet above ground level. These are to be taken at twelve-hour intervals for two weeks during March. You are to report on the results and develop an hypothesis for further testing.

To succeed in this project, you and your partner must assign yourselves a schedule, select a site, and obtain your measuring instrument. You must then set up a table with a calendar or time chart to record your observations. This must be stored carefully so that you do not lose your data. After you have gathered the data, you must look for any patterns in what you have observed (such as differences at the three levels, changes according to time of day, or changes during the two weeks. You will probably need to calculate rates of change. When you write up your report, you will have to be sure to include the following information: names of the researchers, site, days covered, and times of observation. You will need to make a table of your results and you will probably need to make a line graph as well. Then you will have to write up your analysis of the data and the hypothesis you think needs to be established. It could be about lengthening days, about the differences between surface and underground temperatures, about the differences between morning and evening temperatures, or about all three. You will have to include any explanations for your results that might be in your textbook. The writing you have to produce should be impersonal, factual, and in a clear order.

To check whether a piece of science or math writing you have done should be included in your portfolio, ask yourself:

- Are the steps clear?
- Did I omit any necessary material?
- Did I report all the steps in the order I actually followed?
- Is any word unclear?
- Have I included any diagrams or tables that are necessary for my reader?

Literary Writing. Literary writing might include any poems, stories, or plays that you have written either on your own or for a class. This is writing whose primary purpose is to give the reader pleasure in what has been written and in the way that the writing looks, is put together, and sounds. The criteria for your literary writing are the same as those for professional literature. Ask yourself:

- Does the piece make a strong impression?

- Does it make a clear impression?

- Does it hold together well?

- Is it original or does it play with a traditional form or story in an interesting way?

- Is it believable?

- Does it deal with experiences that people think are meaningful and important?

- Does it deserve to be read a second or third time?

Of course, you probably cannot answer these questions yourself. You're probably too close to it. You should get some of your friends to look at what you have written and help you select the pieces that best represent your capabilities.

Some of your literary writing might involve other media. A song, for example, involves both words and music. A video production will involve both the script and the video itself. Include both versions if possible. Consider this example:

You are a member of a musical group that composes its own songs, and you are the lyricist on some of them.

The task you will face is to select the lyrics that you think should go into the portfolio, prepare a clear copy of them, and write a brief explanation of how you came to write them. You should note the date when you wrote them and record the name of the other members of the group, especially the name of the person(s) who wrote the music. You should make several copies and check the format so that they look like lyrics. You should also prepare a tape of the song to go into your portfolio. If it is one piece on a long tape, you will need to include directions as to where to cue the song you want your audience to hear.

Writing Done in the Community. Involving yourself in writing outside of class enables you to show your versatility as a writer. If you belong to an organization or club, consider including in your portfolio minutes, correspondence, purchase records, membership lists, posters, articles, or editorials in the school newspaper. If you have a job, you could include work orders, memoranda, reports, job slips, inventories, or accident reports. You could even use items from home such as journals and diaries, correspondence, record and tape catalogs. Following is an example of community-based writing.

You are a sports reporter on the campus newspaper, and you have covered football, hockey, and tennis.

From this work, you have a chance to select some pieces that show your versatility. Choose pieces that show your range from straight coverage to human interest, from sport to sport, from pieces that describe victory to pieces that describe defeat. Clip these from your paper and make photocopies of them so that you will be ready to arrange them in your portfolio. Don't paste them in a scrapbook unless you have extra loose copies.

Some of these different kinds of writing might involve a combination of text and illustration, or text and music; some may be too large to put in your portfolio. So, you may need to think of some way of recording what you have done. A slide, videotape, or photograph may be a useful way of saving and presenting the work. If the production is complex, you may need to use a videotape or audiotape of the work. These should include some sort of instructions for the viewer or listener as to what part is yours and what part should be the center of attention.

Getting Permission

Remember that some of the writing samples that you have done are not your property, even though you wrote them. If you have written something for an employer, it is best to ask that employer's permission to include a copy of what you wrote. The same rule would apply to writing you have done for a club or organization. Sometimes the organization will not want its name or some of the information in the document to become public knowledge. This would be particularly true of minutes or other records that might cause embarrassment to one or more of the members. Get permission first; if need be, get it in writing. If in doubt, ask. The same rule applies to any research project that involves such things as interviews of other people, photographs, or private property. Your portfolio is a public document; you do not know who will read it.

This means that when you come to consider the final portfolio at the end of the year, you will be looking over everything you have produced to see how it can show each of these aspects of you to your best advantage. But you should begin that thinking early in the course of the semester or the year.

Computer-Managed Portfolios

We wrote this book on a number of Macintosh computers (probably five or six, because we were in three separate places and at least one of us used a portable unit as well as an office machine). It is possible that you will be using a computer for writing as well, perhaps one of your own or a computer from resource center. If so, we suggest that you get your own disk to use as your writing portfolio. Some of the forms and suggestions that are in this book are also available from your instructor on a disk. You may copy any of them and personalize them as you and your instructor think best.

A disk is a good way to think of a portfolio. You can open a separate file for each piece of writing that you are assigned. You may even want to open a separate file for each draft of a long assignment, but that is probably a waste of disk space. If you are using a Macintosh that allows you to create folders on the disk, consider opening a folder for each course as well as one for your personal writing. It is also useful to keep a back-up disk of all your work. You should update the back-up every three weeks or so.

In each of the chapters in this book, we will have some specific suggestions on maintaining your computer-generated writing files and making your final copy, either a final disk that you turn in or a final hard copy. In this chapter, our suggestions concern ways of setting up your writing spaces.

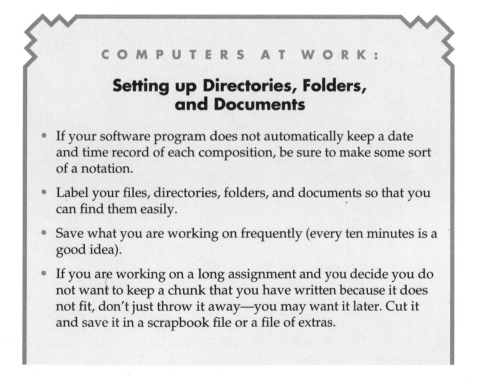

C O M P U T E R S   A T   W O R K :

Setting up Directories, Folders, and Documents

- If your software program does not automatically keep a date and time record of each composition, be sure to make some sort of a notation.

- Label your files, directories, folders, and documents so that you can find them easily.

- Save what you are working on frequently (every ten minutes is a good idea).

- If you are working on a long assignment and you decide you do not want to keep a chunk that you have written because it does not fit, don't just throw it away—you may want it later. Cut it and save it in a scrapbook file or a file of extras.

- If you make an outline first, save the outline as a separate document and then copy it into your text. Check your manual for the best way to use the outlining feature.

- Be sure to put page numbers on each of your documents. A header or footer with the date and a short title is also useful.

- If you networked with others, be sure to label the various contributions so everyone can tell who did what.

- Five minutes of careful planning and filing can save you hours of wandering desperately and searching for a disk or a file you need. We know only too well.

Chapter Summary

What you write and the way you write is a part of your public self, the way you present yourself as a writer, a self-portrait.

To prepare a portfolio, you need to take charge of your writing, both with what you produce and how you produce it. This means setting or negotiating goals and defining the criteria for good writing. It means having a working and presentation portfolio. It means planning, selecting, and putting it all together. It means grouping with others to help each other keep on target. It means looking at all you have written and all you want to write, both in and out of writing class. If you're using a computer, it means setting up your files, directories, and folders for easy access. In short, it means being responsible for your own writing, and for your share in the writing of groups.

Now that you have a sketch of the big picture, go on to the next chapter and see how to get started.

2 Getting Started

Do You Know:

- How to avoid writing well?
- How to interview yourself about your assignments?
- How to get started on, stay with, and finish a project?
- How to use such opening moves as freewriting, mapping, and doubles?

Looking Ahead

Chapter 1 introduced the portfolio concept and the decisions you'll need to make as a writer. In this chapter, you'll see a brief lesson on how to avoid writing well. After that, you'll see that most writers have the same basic problems: getting started, staying with it, and getting finished.

You'll learn to use questions about audience, purpose, and role as a writer to interview yourself about the contexts and directions of your assignments. You'll find directions for and examples of two dozen ways to get started: opening moves. These include such techniques as a writer's notebook, the focus question, metaphor, defining, and comparing and contrasting. With experience, you'll learn what works for you, and then develop your own repertoire of opening moves.

A Brief Lesson

Here is a brief lesson on how to avoid writing well. This will barely take a page. Follow these rules:

1. Don't make a schedule or a deadline for yourself. Write only when you really feel like it, or only at the last minute, for someone else's deadline. Why spoil your spontaneity and freshness by making a job out of it? Everyone knows writing is a talent, anyway; either you have it or you don't.

2. Take no chances on your own. Don't ever dig deeply, discover a new interest, observe something unusual, or head off in a new direction. In fact, if the piece you're working on gets exciting, drop it right away and go back to something safer and superficial.

3. Accept from yourself any excuse you can think up. If you're tired, rest; confused, capitulate; bored, quit; stumped, give up; overwhelmed, drown. If you're not creative with excuses, here are some old standbys: You're not inspired, too busy, too hungry, too blocked. (This last one is especially useful, because no one really knows what it means, but it sounds serious.)

That should cover it. Follow these rules, and the chances are good that you won't write a thing that is really worth reading. Oh, the occasional line or sentence or image might slip out and jolt you from time to time, but you'll learn to avoid most of these surprises and ignore the rest.

If you want to avoid writing well, stop here. You've read far enough. But if you want to write well, you'll want to read on to see the importance of:

*   scheduling and planning and devoting yourself to your work;
*   taking risks and taking charge and taking on a challenge and taking in a hawk's flight and taking a left when the road goes right; and
*   letting nothing stand in your way.

Let's get started.

The Trouble Is . . .

"My three biggest problems with writing? They are getting started, staying with it, and getting finished."

Bill was kidding when he wrote this, but only in part. He did have trouble getting started. It would often be fifteen minutes into the period before he would begin putting words on paper. And there were times when he had trouble continuing. He would get stuck in one place in a piece of writing and not be able to get beyond it, as if there were a boulder blocking the only road out. Finishing was also a problem. Bill didn't have a good sense of what "finished" meant. He could tell when he was out of time or had written the required number of pages, but he couldn't tell if the writing was finished—if the writing could stand by itself and do the job it was supposed to do.

Have you ever had any of these problems? You would be an unusual writer if you haven't. Starting, drafting, and finishing are everyone's problems, in one way or another. Each one of these deceptively simple-sounding categories includes a host of decisions (and indecisions) and a multitude of subproblems that require choices to be made.

However, there are specific strategies you can learn in order to get started, to keep moving, and to get finished. The more techniques or strategies you have in your repertoire, the more adept and versatile a writer you will be. Whether you are working under time pressure (as in an exam situation) or with ample time for experimenting, you can increase your effectiveness as a writer by expanding the ways you know how to work.

Although we will focus on ways to get started in this chapter, we will also spend some time discussing the later stages of writing. Before you decide how to start, it's important to know what you're starting. Like planning a trip, planning a piece of writing often requires some knowledge about your destination.

Setting Up the Job

One of us had this experience:

> The crew had arrived to drill the new well, my daughter informed me. I expected the doorbell to ring, but twenty minutes went by with no ring.
>
> "Elissa," I said, "go around to the back of the house and see what they're doing."
>
> After a few moments, she returned. "I can't tell what they're doing. They're just walking around, spitting and kicking at the ground."
>
> "Okay," I said. "They're getting started. They're setting up the job."
>
> And so they were. They were seeing where the old well was, seeking the best path for the water line to the house, considering distances for various new sites, and finding the best place to set up their drilling rig. Setting up the job.

All of this preliminary work was required because they knew the job wasn't to drill a hole in the ground. The job was to produce a water supply for a family. Drilling a hole in the ground was the way to do that job.

Writing and drilling are not the same activities. You can think of your writing as both the means *and* the end. Writing is the *means* when you are selling a product (through an advertisement), solving a problem (through a complaint letter), explaining your feelings (through a personal note), or winning a contest (through a poem or short story).

Yet writing can also be the *end* in itself. You might try writing fiction just to see if you can complete a short story. Just as you might run to get somewhere quickly or just for the sake of running, you can write as a means and as an end. To get started, you might first consider how a particular piece is a means, an end or both.

So, what should you write? That depends. Here are some possibilities, 60 of them:

journal entry	personal response to literature
directions	research paper
application	interview
personal narrative	character study
radio script	short story
speech	film treatment
interior monologue	stage directions
screenplay	fable or allegory
news report	feature article
oral briefing	lab report
hypothesis	proposal or request
review	analysis
recommendation	peer- or self-evaluation
reflection	magazine article
author profile	song lyrics
billboard design	sonnet
free verse	literary essay
abstract	preview notes
telegram	state of the _____ report
interpretation	progress report
minutes or meeting notes	agenda
editorial	process memo
letter of inquiry	financial report
manual	timeline
appraisal	estimate
brochure	storyboard
acceptance speech	diet or exercise plan
metaphor or analogy	work outline
argument in dialogue	nominating speech
bill for services	resumé or summary

Can you even select a form of writing without knowing something about your audience and purpose? Since the point of writing is hardly ever to produce a particular form, but more often to accomplish a purpose by selecting a form, let's think for a moment about purpose and audience.

Purpose and Audience

To think about purpose, we have to think about audience, as well. Following is a list of questions to ask yourself as a writer. These will help you not only to get started, but also to get started in a useful direction. When you have an assignment to complete, or as a way to generate one of your own, jot down answers to these questions:

THINKING ABOUT . . .

Audience and Purpose

Audience
- Who is my audience?
- How many levels of audience am I trying to reach?
- What do they know about this topic?
- What do they know about me?
- How will they evaluate my work?
- What social, cultural, and personal contexts exist?

Purpose
- What responses do I want from each level of audience?
- What do I want each to think? To do?
- What direct and indirect effects am I looking for?
- What do I know about producing these effects in readers?
- How will I evaluate my work—how will I measure the effects?

Role as Writer
- How do I want to come across as a writer?
- What is my reputation, and what will I make of myself?
- What is my stance: Authority? Discoverer? Something else?

- What tone and degree of formality will be appropriate?
- What part of larger "conversations" is this writing?

Topic

- What—exactly—am I going to write about?
- What subtopics, references, and comparisons will help define the topic?
- What form(s) will give proper shape to this topic for this audience?

Conditions

- How much time do I have to produce this piece of writing?
- How many drafts or revisions will be possible?
- What resources are at my disposal? Texts? People? Experiences?
- How long should the writing be? How long should it take to read?
- What is the reading situation—in what contexts will it be read?

Answering the context questions will lead you to answers to these payoff questions about your work:

- What am I hired to do?
- What am I selling with this piece? With this portfolio?

As a writer, it is your responsibility to answer all of these questions and contextualize the writing for yourself and for the reader. No editor will do this for you, and an instructor who does all this for you has done too much. A good part of the writing process is making decisions, and you need to make your own. You've got to drop the training wheels if you're really going to ride the bicycle. That involves setting up the job yourself, even if you're working with a topic or assignment from someone else. If you want to be articulate, fluent, flexible, and independent, start by being independent. The rest will come with work and experience.

When you have some answers to the questions we've just looked at, you've already solved the problem of how to get started. You're also in a position to start making decisions about the forms your writing might take. You have an idea about your destination. The destination may change as the writing progresses, but at least you have a direction to start in.

Opening Moves

So start. Do it. Make text. Write. The techniques explained in the rest of this chapter will give you many ways to make enough text to work with. After you write a page or two of text, you can become your own first audience and start to react to the piece as a reader and a writer. You can read passages aloud and hear the flow and rhythm of your language. A later chapter will show you ways to work with the products of these opening moves.

These opening moves are ways to begin mining the richness of experience and thought that lies in your memory. They are ways to get beyond the superficial and automatic expressions that first come to mind. They are techniques to learn how to use, and techniques to *remember* to use. Runners learn stretching exercises not just as exercises, but also as ways to prepare for the run. Developing as a writer requires that you work on your habits, as well as on your knowledge and practice. Think of the techniques you see in this book as tools to use, rather than as tricks you can perform.

When you are trying an opening move, make the most of your time. Remember that 25 minutes of writing will give you several pages to work with. The same time spent getting your pencils ready, straightening out the desk, and worrying about the exact place to start will probably make you 25 minutes older but no closer to starting the writing. (Please note that we do not consider daydreaming a waste of time, particularly if you do it with a pencil handy.)

"Move" is the key word. If you're lost in the woods, you should stay put and wait to be rescued. If you're lost in a writing, you have to work your way out, by writing. No one is coming to rescue you, and there are a million ways out.

Here are a few of them. These first strategies generally begin with a topic and explore that topic in one or more ways. The form of the thinking may be less important than the topic and subtopics discovered through the exploration.

Each technique or opening move is followed by an example and an exercise. The examples were written as first drafts by students like you. We gave them an early version of this chapter and asked them to try the opening moves. Even though the examples have been typed, they are drafts, not finished writings that have been revised and edited.

Writer's Notebook

The easiest way to get started is to be started already. A basic law of physics says that a body in motion tends to stay in motion. As a writer, keep moving. Write every day. If you do, you're unlikely to experience much of the fabled "writer's block" or "terror of the blank page." Your page will never be blank.

And, when you're moving, you can use your own momentum to pull you along. Racers will often slide in behind the front-runner to be pulled along in the slipstream created by the leader's motion. This maneuver is called *drafting,* a word also used to mean developing the first version of a piece of writing. If you're always working on something, always on the move as a writer, you can slip in behind your own working momentum and let it pull you through the work.

Don't just work on assignments or projects given to you. Keep a notebook or journal or diary or log of ideas, impressions, artful phrases, new forms, interesting names, irritating circumstances, oddities, and anything else that strikes you.

TABLE 2.1 WRITER'S NOTEBOOK POSSIBILITIES

NAME	PURPOSE AND METHOD	FREQUENCY OF USE
Learning Log	Record progression of learning in a course over extended time—each new formula, technique, strategy, or other type of understanding	Daily, weekly, or by project
Problem File	Record difficulties experienced in assignments, homework, tests, lectures, demonstrations	When teacher directs; when problems arise
Discovery Book	Make predictions, hypotheses, explanations, tentative conclusions for topic under investigation	Any time during class, reading, or home-work
Assessment Profile	Goals or expectations, quarterly, mid-year, annual assessments of own work according to established criteria	Beginnings/ends of marking periods and courses
Project Journal	Plan and record all stages of a project from topic, conducting research, drafting, revising, redrafting, editing, presenting or publishing	Daily for length of project
Study Guide	Collect and organize information for later study and review for final exam, paper, or presentation	Guide or section for each major topic or work
Reading Log	Record readings and comments in double-entry form: Quote from reading on left; on right, questions, comments, associations, evaluations, speculations	Daily during any reading or research project

What if nothing strikes you? Then get busy and start looking. Break through the trance of day-to-day existence (you don't really have to notice anything to make your way to school or work, do you?). Go to new places for observations. Go to familiar places and find five new things to think and write about. Ask questions. Make hypotheses. Make text. In your other classes, use writing to help you learn and to help you learn to write. Table 2.1 gives some other notebook possibilities for your science, history, math, and other courses.

Example 2.1 is a notebook entry based on a simple observation.

EXAMPLE 2.1 WRITER'S NOTEBOOK—AN OBSERVATION

Something I found interesting today was in the movie Robin Hood. The part I found particularly eye-catching was when Robin was talking to the woodsmen, trying to unite them against the sheriff. Here Robin said, "I make you no promises, save one . . .". I was drawn to when Robin says "save one." This was strange because we usually don't hear someone use this in spoken English. This seems to be a part of what has become forgotten words and phrases in standard English.

—Austin Willoughby

EXERCISE 2.1 STARTING A WRITER'S NOTEBOOK

To get started, try to write three beautiful sentences. Write the same idea in three different ways. Write a 200-word sentence. Write 20 short sentences. Play with rhythm and rhyme. Later, go back to what you've written and play with the text you've made. Find a key word on one page and a key word on another, and develop a link between them.

Undirected Writing or Freewriting

Freewriting is just what it sounds like: Verbal wandering, but wandering usually done at some speed for four to five minutes. Do this by simply stringing words and sentences together until the time is up. You might start with a word, phrase, or concept if you have a particular topic ("nationalism," say, or "structure," or "food chain," or "transmission," or "tempo," or "technique," or "format," or "health") to write about.

Don't look back, don't edit, and write as fast as you can. When you're finished, go back and read it to find a point of focus, or at least a glimmer of a place to start. If you can write half a page in four to five minutes, you will probably produce some useful and interesting text, a way to get into your topic. If your first attempt is unsuccessful, try again.

If you like to write with a partner or group, you might exchange writings at this point and each tell the other what you see in the text. These responses should be informative but not critical:

"I want to know more about this . . ."
"This line or sentence seems to be your topic . . ."
"You're making me think that . . ."

When you get your writing back, you will have had some help in finding your real topic (or letting the topic find you). Example 2.2 shows a student's attempt at freewriting.

EXAMPLE 2.2 FREEWRITING

From the time of birth up until the age 14 my life was a bit of a roller coaster: six months here, six months there. Sometimes I used to wonder where I was. You see, my father is an accountant and the majority of his clients live in New York City. So every year when infamous "tax season" came we were off & moving.

Truthfully, I didn't really mind it all that much. I had two sets of friends, & boy, what a greeting you get when you come back after six months. I used to live in New Jersey & my dad would commute into the city. When I was young I loved country trees, but as I grew older I enjoyed the malls & the busy way of life in Jersey.

Just when I was waiting to decide which high school to go

to my parents (a very exciting issue) sprung the news on me (where I lived not many people went to public high school.) They had decided to permanently move upstate. Well, I didn't take it well. Why were they doing this to me? I didn't want to move up to the boonies for the rest of my life.

    The first full year I went to school up here was the worst. I didn't care about my grades or my friends. I barely cared about myself. I got over it, though. I enjoy each & every day I spend in the country. With my 30 acres & horses. But as soon as graduation arrives: I'm out of here!

—Paige Asdoorian

EXERCISE 2.2 FREEWRITING

If you have been assigned a topic, use a key word from that topic for this activity. If you have no topic you must write about, pick one you want to write about. Start with a word or idea you want to write about and write without stopping for four to five minutes. Then read your work (or ask another person to read it) to find a point of focus. (Exercise 2.3, which follows, will show you how to take another step with the text you produced in this activity.)

Directed Writing

Freewriting is called "free" because it has no particular direction. It needs no particular direction. It can start anywhere and end anywhere. It does not have to make a point or solve a problem. Most of your writing assignments, however, require your work to have more direction. The technique explained here, directed writing, can be a continuation of freewriting. The text you produced during freewriting can be given some shape. Directed writing can also be used to explore a specific topic or assignment you have been given by an instructor.

    Example 2.3 shows a writer starting with an undirected writing (another name for a freewriting) and then directing herself to an answer to a specific question. You can see that the undirected writing raised the question she wanted to answer in the directed writing.

EXAMPLE 2.3 UNDIRECTED WRITING LEADING TO DIRECTED WRITING

On a wall of the classroom is a glass case that is very interesting. In this glass case are papers that are arranged in a spiral pattern. Each one of the papers looks like an essay or story. They are written by students in a different class. In the center of this spiral pattern of works is a poem that is very interesting.

The paper in the case is black, and all the white papers are contrasted on the black background. The case is very interesting to a plain classroom.

Directed Writing: What Does the Poem Tell Me About Poetry?

Poems are very interesting pieces of literature. They seem to be able to make one feel what the poets are saying. Sometimes a poem can make you just so depressed by what it is trying to say.

A poem does not have to be in any certain way. Almost anything can be a poem, songs can be poems.

A poem that I once saw talked about something that seemed very true. I feel that if you don't tell a person anything they will never learn anything. On the other hand, if you tell someone something they might find out too much. This is exactly what the poem said.

—Jennifer Herrick

EXERCISE 2.3 DIRECTED WRITING

Take the point of focus either from an assignment you've been given or from an undirected writing you want to work on further. For four to five minutes, explore the topic from a particular point of view, slant, or perspective. If you started with "nationalism," you might now go to "dangers of nationalism" or something more directed: "importance of structure" or "threats to the food chain" or "purposes of the transmission" or "varying tempo" or "brush technique" or "racquet technique" or "balanced format" or "diet's effects on health."

When you are working with an abstraction that is particularly evasive, you might start with a free writing, and then follow it immediately with one (or more) focused free writings to bring the topic into increasingly sharp definition.

If a partner responded to your writing, pick up on that response. Bring the topic into sharper focus through your elaboration. You're not trying to produce an essay, so let the writing go where it goes. No editing.

Word Association

You probably have played (or have seen played) a word association game of some type. The technique of word association makes for an interesting opening move because it lets you explore the intellectual and emotional reactions you have to words. You will find that your pattern of reactions is unique. Although ten people might give almost identical dictionary definitions of the word "family," their ten word associations would show significant differences. It is these personal differences in responses that word association helps you to discover.

Example 2.4 presents two columns. The list in the left-hand column gives associations for the words in the title of a play. On the right is the writer's discovery from the associations.

EXAMPLE 2.4 WORD ASSOCIATION

The Effects of Gamma Rays on Man-in-the-Moon Marigolds

chemistry—gamma rays	I have discovered
green cheese (in the moon)	that this title leads
Easter (marigolds)	me to believe that
daisies—flowers	the story will be
science-fiction—future	in the future

astronaut—outer space
rocketships—to get to the moon
nuclear war—gamma rays
atomic bomb—gamma rays
gardens—flowers
fertilizer—to grow
stars—outer space
sun—rays
radiation—rays

science-fiction
about some weird
experiment with
flowers that
will affect the
world.

—Meeghan Smith

EXERCISE 2.4 WORD ASSOCIATION

As a place to start, write a key word (or two) about the topic you've been assigned or have chosen to write about. If you're writing about a literary text, you might use the title, the first few words, or the last few words of the piece. In a vertical list below the key word, quickly list 15–20 words that come to mind when you think of the key word. Try to do this in two to three minutes. Then, for each word on the list you generated, try to write a few words that connect with that word. Write these next to each word.

Finally, look at the mass of words you have created and look for points of focus and connections. See what you have discovered about your own views of this subject. Ask a partner to have a look and give you a response.

Doodling or Sketching

Your visual thinking can help your verbal thinking. In this opening move, you draw or sketch or write whatever comes to mind as you listen, watch, or think. You may produce (in text, picture, or combination) a starting point for a writing that is a personal reflection, an attitude, or a perception. Example 2.5 begins with a poem, but turns into a sketch.

EXAMPLE 2.5 DOODLING OR SKETCHING: A POEM THAT TURNS INTO A SKETCH

The Burn of its color, Sharpness of light
casts a shadow upon our extinction.

The passion of its burn foregoes all might
A shadow that the provider provides,
The Ray that stabs into each soul.
Contrasting images which appear.
A routine of sensations, it fairly plays its rule
A hate to some, another's fear.
Through sunglass eyes and ceramic heart
Nothing appears as it should.
If you hate, you hate. Love always prevails.
My footprints still, the Last sparkling Ray
The feeling saved. Until the dawn of a new day.

—Kris Badman

EXERCISE 2.5 DOODLING OR SKETCHING

Relax and clear your mind. Let your pencil start to move on the paper as your mind wanders. As you continue, you may notice a pattern or shape evolving in the doodling or sketch. Go with it. Continue drawing what you seem to have started drawing. If you start to write words, that's fine. Continue writing and/or sketching for four to five minutes or until you notice something taking shape. This activity might result in a whole work (of writing or drawing) or just the beginning of something else.

Telling a Story

The story is one of the most powerful and compelling modes or forms of writing. People have probably been telling (and reading) stories to you since you were a young child. You've probably told a few yourself. As an opening move, telling a story is an easy way to get started, even if the writing you eventually do does not take narrative form. One power of the story is that it can organize seemingly unrelated events for you. Another is that it causes you to fill in gaps as you try to keep the story going, thus finding in yourself some ideas you didn't know you had.

Example 2.6 is the result of an assignment to write about an important event. Once he started, the writer quickly produced four or five pages of story—it poured out of him. We show you here only the opening paragraph, a line from the middle, and a line from the end.

EXAMPLE 2.6 TELLING A STORY

At the pep rally in the auditorium on Friday afternoon, the Canajoharie football team was pumped to stomp all over the unbeaten Whitehall team we would be playing at Homecoming. We all decided to go out together as a team to Ponderosa and enjoy the night before the big game. We ate, laughed, and talked about the possible outcome of the game and wondered if our young, up-and-coming team could defeat a team with a 4–0 record. After we finished eating, we went to the arcade and then went home early so we would be well rested for the big game. Whitehall led 12–8 at the half, but final score 24–12, Canajoharie.

—Darin Bowerman

EXERCISE 2.6 TELLING A STORY

Start narrating a story that begins with a person, place, event, or time that is of interest to you or relevant to the topic assigned by your instructor. Write in detail, even though you may seem to be making up most of what you write. Some of this imaginary knowledge will turn out to be useful—maybe even true.

Start in the middle or at the beginning or at the end, whatever works best for you. Write for 15 to 20 minutes or so without looking back at what you've written. You may wish to try to reach an ending of some sort, or you might get interested in developing one particular part of the story. It may help you to write to an audience you can picture: your younger sister, a district attorney, a carriage driver. Read what you've written and see if you have developed an interesting topic, character, sentence, or story line.

Another way to start is to take a sentence from a book or a poem you like. It should be a sentence that contains an action.

Sailing in the bathtub, the goat landed on the roof.

Take that sentence and make it the climax of the story. That means you have to write the exposition and rising action that leads up to the climactic sentence. Then you have to write a resolution that ties things up.

Or you could make it the first sentence. Or the last sentence.

---

20 Questions

When you are given a topic to research and write about, ask 20 questions to help you set a research agenda. For each category, try to work toward more and more specific and detailed questions, the kind an investigator or cross-examiner might ask, the kind you'd have to ask if you were playing *20 questions*. The more detailed your questions, the more they will help you to direct your own research beyond the obvious. Ask questions in the following categories: who, what, where, when, why, and how. Example 2.7 is a response to a college application essay topic that asked the writer to "Tell us something important about yourself." Her opening move was to ask 20 questions to help her decide what to write about. Her next move will be to select the most interesting questions and then write answers to them.

EXAMPLE 2.7 20 QUESTIONS

1. Who are you? (descriptive thoughts)
2. What do you like to do in your spare time?
3. Where do you go on weekends?

4. How would you describe your life? Would it be hectic, slow-paced, easygoing etc.?
5. Why do you like or dislike yourself?
6. What things do you think stand out about yourself?
7. Why do you think they stand out?
8. Who inspires you?
9. What are some important things you want to talk about in school?
10. What is most important to you? Material or activity-wise.
11. Where would you go, if you could, to help other people?
12. When was there a time that's most memorable to you?
13. What aspect of your life keeps you going, or inspires you the most?
14. How would you describe yourself differently to an adult than to your classmate?
15. When was a time that occurs to you that was your most embarrassing moment?
16. How do you think you changed from when you were younger to now?
17. Why do you think this change has occurred?
18. How do you see yourself, if you move at the same pace of life, in 10 years?
19. What are some goals you have set for yourself?
20. How will you attempt to achieve these goals?

—Jen Wilder

EXERCISE 2.7 20 QUESTIONS

At the top of your paper, write a name for the topic you will be exploring. Down the left-hand margin, write

1. Who . . .
2. Who . . .
3. Who . . .
4. Who . . .

Continue with three or four question leads beginning with "What," "When," "Where," and "How." Start with any question that comes to mind first. Move to different categories as one question leads to another. Work toward more and more specific questions. Ask as many questions as you can. You don't have to stop at 20. When you are finished, you will have created a research and/or writing agenda for yourself.

Concept Mapping

A concept map, like any other map, is a representation of a territory. However, the "territory" shown by a concept map is not a place but a network of ideas. The map attempts to show in two dimensions the relationships between and among ideas. In a way, it's a visual outline of the ideas that might later appear in a work of writing. Some writers of fiction use story maps to work out relationships among elements such as characters, settings, and events.

Example 2.8 shows a writer's exploration of what goes on in her English class.

EXAMPLE 2.8 CONCEPT MAPPING

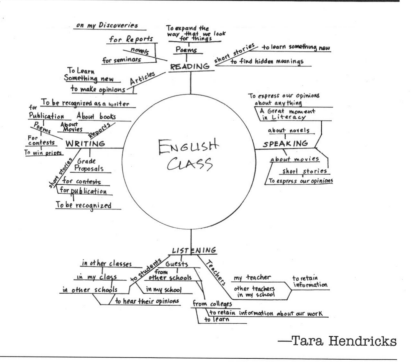

—Tara Hendricks

EXERCISE 2.8 CONCEPT MAPPING

Begin by drawing a two-inch circle in the middle of a blank page. In the center, write your topic. Then, draw a few rays from the circle out toward the edges of the paper, a sunburst effect. On each ray, write a subtopic or aspect of the main topic. Draw branches from each ray for yet smaller subdivisions or associations. Continue until you've filled the page with topics and subtopics, and you will have explored your present knowledge of this topic in some detail.

Arrange topics or details spatially in ways that make sense to you, and then explain your arrangement. These "arrangements" can be drawn or completed by writing connections between and among the topics. If the topic were sandpaper, for example, #80, #220, and #360 sandpapers might be arranged in order of coarseness or in order of use. Items might be connected by location, use, cause and effect, time order, or other kinds of logic. Remember that your map is an interpretation or construction. Another person could make a very different map of the same territory.

Focus Question

A focus question must be a *big* question—a question that brings together all the subquestions and related issues of a topic you're working with. To start off, you might ask yourself the question, "What happened?" or "What is happening?" Ask the question as you:

- put spin (or spit, if you like) on a ball;

- play vibrato;

- toss an object into the air and let it drop to the floor;

- light a cigarette and watch it burn;

- draw a normal (or bell) curve;

- flip a coin five times and record the results;

- hit a function or command keystroke on a computer;

- knock flakes of rust from an old nail; or

- exaggerate the rhythm of a poem or song.

Example 2.9 shows how asking such a question can lead you to notice something you hadn't noticed before.

EXAMPLE 2.9 FOCUS QUESTION

When I do something, I like to know why it had the result it did. For instance, something that makes music so much more interesting is to use vibrato. It really is a simple thing. You just rapidly rock your finger on the string making the note go in and out of tune rapidly. It is something that you would think would make the song bad but it actually makes it sound better. It gives it a personality, a character all its own.

Note: I picked a topic and asked myself the question, "What is happening?" and why. It seems that I never thought about vibrato until I was asked to.

—Kelly Van Gorder

EXERCISE 2.9 FOCUS QUESTION

Develop your own focus question. You might use a photograph, painting, headline, film clip, or object as a focal point. Placing side by side two objects, photos, or headlines is another effective way to start: an NRA "Right to Bear Arms" poster next to a headline about a drive-by shooting, for example. As an opening move, the focus question takes you to a central issue about the topic.

"What If ?" Reasoning

"What if" reasoning can be useful if you are working on a presentation, discussion, essay, or research assignment. You simply ask "What if" and write a three- to four-sentence answer that suggests an outcome and explains why it should or might result. You can distinguish between projections and predictions with this technique. You might project what *could* happen, in an open-ended speculation, or you might predict what *should* happen.

"What if land couldn't be owned?" "What if you established these points in a different quadrant?" "What if the rate and type of mutations could be controlled?" "What if you wrote a piece in 5/4 time?" "What if you rotate this 90 degrees?" "What if the law of averages was suspended for a weekend?" "What if you put this in the oven without thawing it first?" "What if you put underspin on the ball?"

Anyone who has watched a magician knows how important the "why" of the answer is. It is at least as important as the "what" because it requires that you pay attention to cause and effect as well as speculate about possibilities. As curious people, we usually want to know *why* or *how* something happens as much as we want to know *what* happens. Use this technique to begin working on a class presentation or discussion, or a homework, essay, or research assignment.

Example 2.10 comes from a science assignment that required "what if?" thinking.

EXAMPLE 2.10 "WHAT IF" REASONING

What if cold air rose instead of warm air? This question was part of my Physics homework and it is an open ended question which the student must answer. The answer to the question is that there really is no answer because the question is only asking "what if," which leaves only speculation on the students part of what would happen if the situation was possible.

If warm air no longer rose but instead cold air did, we would never experience going into a hot attic but instead what used to be the cold basement would be warm. If warm air sank below the cold air the weight of the heavy, cooler air would work as a blanket, trapping the warmer air in near the surface and in effect raising the temperature on the surface.

These are only speculations and ideas of what the outcome would be if a natural law was changed. We cannot tell whether the answer is correct because we have never experienced a time when cold air rose above warm air.

—Austin Willoughby

EXERCISE 2.10 "WHAT IF?" REASONING

Start by identifying a concept or relationship you want to explore. Any subject will do. "What if?" thinking is involved in every course you are now taking. After you identify the topic, select a "law" or "truth" or "rule" about that topic and turn it around or stand it on its head. Start with, "What if . . ." and write the reverse of the law. Then speculate as to what would happen in those circumstances. This exploration of the inverted law (or truth or rule) will help you to see why the law is important and how it functions as a law.

Process Memo

The device known as a process memo is especially useful for understanding your problem-solving or thinking process. It causes you to pay attention to the steps you follow. This technique may be most useful with a problem that is complex and difficult, since this is a case where steps need the most attention. Example 2.11 began as a process memo, as the writer recorded the steps she followed, and then evolved into a set of directions for writing a process memo.

EXAMPLE 2.11 PROCESS MEMO

Process memos should be an important part of writing. Many times they are overlooked but, to me, they are of great importance.

When you do a process memo, it is important to write down all the steps you took when doing your piece, such as where you were when you did it and how you came up with the idea. Then, go through the steps from your draft, all the way to the final copy. Explain the reasons for revisions, if any, and what you learned after you were finished. This helps a writer to keep track of her work.

It is good to explain your work, what you did and why. This will not only help the reader to understand your work, but also it will help you for the next time you write. Process memos lay precedents of guidelines for future assignments.

—Nora Sanson

EXERCISE 2.11 PROCESS MEMO

Select a problem you need to solve or an activity you want to understand better or improve in some way. A demonstration speech or a writing explaining a process would be ideal assignments for which to use this opening move. As you work on the problem or do the activity, jot down in as few words as possible the steps you are taking. In effect, you are writing a lab report about yourself. When you finish the activity and the writing, you will have a record not only of where you went wrong, but also of where you went *right*. Read your process memo as you would look at an instant replay to see how to improve your technique, or to see if you notice something that you hadn't noticed before.

Support It/Deny It

With the "support it/deny it" technique, you are asked to be an advocate for two sides of an issue or story. After you find evidence to show that "A is true," you find evidence to show that "A is not true." When you are finished with this technique, you will have considered both sides of the issue and will know more about it than if you had considered it from only one view. The object of this opening move is not to see which side wins, but to develop as much understanding as you can of the topic. With any complex issue, you should remember that "both sides of the story" is still not the whole story.

Example 2.12 is based on the statement, "The environment must be protected at all costs." The writer says "Yes, because . . ." and then "No, because . . ." as she examines the issue from two sides.

EXAMPLE 2.12 SUPPORT IT/DENY IT

Support It:

The environment has to be protected at any cost. Right now is the time to start protecting the environment, not twenty years from now. If we wait until later there may not be an environment to protect. The environment is our society that we live in. Without this society we can't live. The environment gives us the air that we breathe and the sites we enjoy. The environment means more to us than just what we need to live. The environment gives us security and joy. We spend more time in the environment than we do anywhere else. Some people may work in the environment. Food for people could not be produced without the environment, which would mean that the world would not exist without having a stable and well-kept environment for everyone to live in. The main point of this is that the world would not exist without the environment as a whole. People can't survive, can't live, can't eat without the environment. The environment may not always be kind, but it's all we have to live with and it should be protected like anything else in our lives.

Deny It:

The environment does not have to be protected at any cost. Right now the government and the people of the world do not have the patience, time and money to deal with the environment. At this time the environment isn't the most important part of our lives for us; it's just getting through the days, rather than having to deal with what may or may not happen in twenty years. Cities and countries have problems getting people to recycle. It is seen as a nuisance for people and we just don't want to deal with it. Maybe in time we will but now we are just going to go our own way and see what happens.

—Krista Caldwell

EXERCISE 2.12 SUPPORT IT/DENY IT

Begin by creating an arguable statement relevant to your topic. Below are some examples.

- U.S. borders should be closed to any further immigration.
- The U.S. should intervene in areas torn by civil war.
- Alcohol use should not be regulated.
- _____ music isn't music at all.
- _____ is one of the greatest _____ ever written/composed/painted/built . . .

For five to ten minutes, write support—actual or tentative—for the statement as it is worded. Then, become an advocate for the other side, and spend the next three to four minutes marshaling evidence to deny or refute the statement. You will have an investment in exploring two sides (there may be more) of the main issue you want to deal with. If you wish, a third writing can follow. Take a moment to read what you have written as a "hired" advocate for the two sides. Then, begin writing what you actually believe about the issue. By asking yourself to "see" two sides, you give yourself a chance to develop your own ideas, as well as these two positions, with greater clarity and definition.

Inside and Outside Perspectives

With this technique, you write from two points of view. First, you write a view of a topic or issue or event from the inside, as one of the participants. You write in first person, and you do not worry about the scientific or historical accuracy of what you write. You leave that for later research.

Then you write another view of the same subject, but from an external perspective: that of an observer, commentator, analyst, or reporter. Write this view in first or third person. Give this "person" a specific role. "The queen's hairdresser, witnessing the queen's beheading" is much more specific than "a witness at an execution." You might want to write from more than two perspectives. The power of this opening move is that it highlights differences. Using this technique will help you to avoid over-simplifications such as "Everybody hates war."

The first part of Example 2.13 is from a boy's point of view as he plays in the park. The second part is the view of an old woman who observes him.

EXAMPLE 2.13 INSIDE/OUTSIDE PERSPECTIVES

First perspective: A Boy and His Pet in the Park

There we were in the middle of the Amazon Jungle, just me and my ferocious Lion, Spot. The sound of wild man-eating animals all around us. But I'm not afraid because I'm Barry the Great. Suddenly a Wild-eyed native jumped in front of us and tried to attack us. But with my Super Human Strength I picked up a huge boulder and threw it at the native, and It ran away.

Another perspective: An Old Woman Sitting in the Park Feeding the Pigeons

What a beautiful, relaxing day. I love to sit here on my bench in the park just absorbing the day's beauty and warmth.

"Here Little Pigeon, come here, Floyd."

Hmm. What's this? A boy and his dog. How sweet. Those were the days, young and not a care in the world. What the . . . Well that little whippersnapper just threw a rock at that poor little girl over there! Boy, I guess times are changing.

—Bobby Bascomb

EXERCISE 2.13 INSIDE/OUTSIDE PERSPECTIVES

Topics or subjects of any kind can be explored with this technique. After you identify your topic, select at least two distinct perspectives from which to write. Each perspective should be specific. Let yourself "see" this narrator, just as you would develop a character in detail. Consider age, gender, ethnic background, religion, family, work life, attitudes, and important earlier events. When you have the narrator clearly in mind, tell the story or describe the scene from that narrator's perspective.

Then create another narrator and write from another perspective. Consider, again, what would this narrator see? How would he or she interpret what is seen? How would it be reported?

20 Opening Lines

"None of them knew the color of the sky." This opening line (from "The Open Boat," by Stephen Crane) is interesting because it raises many questions: Who were they? Where were they? Why couldn't they, or didn't they, see the sky? The aim of this opening move is to write not one, but 20 opening lines. Because the first sentence raises questions, this sentence will give you, as a writer, ideas on how to proceed. As you write these opening lines, don't worry about which one you will eventually use. Just write as quickly as you can, and let your mind wander as you write, seeking different angles on and details about your topic. A variation of this technique is to write 20 closing lines or last sentences.

The example that follows shows you 20 possible openings for an auto-biography.

EXAMPLE 2.14 20 OPENING LINES FOR AN AUTOBIOGRAPHY

1. It all started on a dark night on August 26th.
2. I SCREAMED. It was so cold!
3. It was the middle of the night. My mother was getting stomach pains.
4. My life story starts when I'm 20. I had a boring childhood.
5. Mom took the test. It was pink!!
6. My aunt held me in her arms as she handed me to my mother.
7. One silent tear ran down her cheek, when in her arms was laid the girl she always wanted.
8. My first sense . . . Smell, hospitals stink!
9. The farthest back my memory goes is to my 4th birthday. My Uncle Johnny . . .
10. I'm sick of eating second-hand food. Maybe there's a candy bar where that light is.
11. Who is that deadbeat with the video camera? Daddy who?
12. Why was I put in a crib? Baby Prison.

13. Why is it that every time I open my mouth, something comes out of it?

14. I have never seen a lady so beautiful as the one who held me tight in that smelly hospital.

15. My first lie was when I knocked over a plant in the living room and blamed it on my dog. This started my life of bank robbery.

16. I am a test tube baby. . .

17. Watch out world, Here I come!

18. It was a miracle, a Glory of Life.

19. I got my first chemistry set when I was eight. Who would have thought I would find the cure for AIDS.

20. My greatest inspiration was my mother. When I was five . . .

—Kris Badman

EXERCISE 2.14 20 OPENING LINES

Write 20 sentences that could be the opening lines of the story or paper or other piece you want to (or have to) write. Write them quickly and from as many different places in your mind as you can. When you've finished, you can select the best one and continue writing by answering the questions raised in that first sentence. You might even discover that, with some reorganization, you've written a good part of the piece. Other good sentences from this activity might fit elsewhere in the piece.

Making a Movie

Peter Elbow, a teacher and writer, talks about "making the movie in your head," something a reader does in response to a written piece. As the reader tells the writer what the movie was like, the writer gets a better idea of the effects of the work he or she produced. We will use this technique in a different way—to get you to see the movie in your own head. You won't need a camera, just a storyboard.

A storyboard is a device used to plan audiovisual productions such as films and television presentations. A completed one looks like a comic book or strip. This device lets you think visually, aurally, and verbally at the same time. It also requires you to make decisions about distance, angle, transition, pace, and other elements of writing that are easier to see than to visualize. To complete one card or frame of a storyboard, you have to make at least a dozen decisions. Don't worry about beauty; what you want to be sure of is that you clearly indicate the camera angle and distance for each "shot." Include the notes for any sound track (narration, dialogue, music, voice-over, sound effects) and the length of shot and transition to next shot (cut, fade, etc.).

It may not be possible to hand in the storyboard as a completed assignment, but making it will certainly help you to see, hear, and think about the treatment you want for the topic. Think of it as a bridge to take you from verbal thinking to audiovisual thinking—and back again.

Example 2.15 is just a beginning. The writer has sketched visuals and added narrative to show five stages of an event. Notice that she has chosen different camera angles and distances. She has varied the amount of narration on each frame, giving you some idea of the pace of the work. If the work she has done so far is enough to give her a firm sense of her writing, then she can move on. If not, she can keep working and make decisions about the length of each shot, transition from shot to shot, music and other sound effects, setting and costume, and other elements.

EXAMPLE 2.15 STORYBOARD

The 400 Meter Dash

It was June 4, 1993, when the 400 Meter Dash was announced over the loud speakers.

The six of us set ourselves in our starting blocks, pinned in our lanes. The commands sounded and there was a bang.

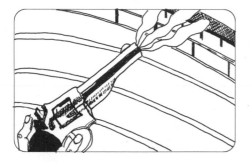

The suffocating smell of the gunpowder filled my nose and mouth as I turned the first, then the second corner.

My legs were tight, reddish; my mouth, chapped, but still I ran head-to-head with the best of the best 'till the end, until I died.

I remember nothing more except for the relieving sight of a fellow racer helping me walk off the track and the scarlet-colored face of my coach as I approached him and asked . . .

"What was my time?"

—Tara Hendrick

EXERCISE 2.15 MAKING A MOVIE

Create a storyboard for the piece you're working with. You can begin with an idea or topic, a piece of writing from another opening move, or a complete draft of a writing. First, make a quick list of parts or stages or features of the work ("The 400 Meter Dash" had five parts). Next, sketch a picture for each part. What do you want the viewer to see? From what distance? What angle or point of view? Let the pictures tell the story.

Next, add sound track: narration, dialogue, music, and sound effects. Write these elements on the corresponding cards or frames. Next, consider pace and transitions. How many seconds should each shot last? How will you get from one shot to another? Will you cut directly from shot #1 to shot #2? Fade out on #1 and fade in on #2?

Before this opening move turns into an opening movie, let's remember that we can go back to verbal thinking and expression at any time. The purpose of making the movie was to help make the writing: to see in pictures what was hard to "see."

Doubles

This opening move requires you to do two of something quickly. You write two quick first drafts that are different from each other in form, voice, time perspective, or intended audience. Why are two drafts better than one? For the same reason that conversation might be more interesting than talking to yourself: different kinds of comparison, contrast, tension, and harmony are all possible. You can decide how the drafts will differ before you start, or you can start one and wait for an idea for the second to come as you write the first.

In Example 2.16, the writer explains in the note at the end that she had the second idea while she was working on the first.

EXAMPLE 2.16 DOUBLES

A.

Almost everything I do defines who I am. Just the way I react to a situation shows what I believe, and in turn, who I am. Almost anyone I come in contact with can get a general idea of who I am, but I think that their perception of me is wrong. You cannot base your opinion on things like me playing an instrument or what sports I participate in. While those things may influence me they do not form me as a person. Things like the fact that I procrastinate, and I am not very good at expressing my true feelings towards people because I don't like to let people get too close to me are more me than those little things that are really insignificant.

B.

I, as a person, am defined not only by the things I do, but also by the things I don't do. I view myself as a selfish person. I usually do not do things that are inconvenient for me, and I do not often take other people's feelings into consideration when I make my decisions. I also do not work up to my potential. This fact is going to affect the rest of my life. Another thing that will affect the rest of my life is that I do not have a long attention span. Although I am working on trying to fix these things that are negative, they have still shaped my life and formed the person that I am, which in turn forms the person that I will grow to be.

Note: For 20 minutes I made a list of all of the things that I do. It began as a list of things that really meant nothing, things that everyone knows. It later became a list with depth. I then made a list of the things that I don't do.

—Kelly Van Gorder

EXERCISE 2.16 DOUBLES

Choose an assignment or topic and write in two forms. Write an obituary and a sonnet, a letter to the editor and a historical account, a character study and a palmist's predictions, or any other combination that creates some tension or dissonance for you to work with.

Or write two blind drafts of the same thing. Give yourself 20 minutes, say, to write the first version of your essay on "patriotism" or "the importance of electricity" or whatever is your topic. Write feverishly and do not look back at what you've written. Then start another draft, not really as a continuation of the other. Start somewhere else. Write with the same concentration and for the same amount of time. Then read both and see what you can do with the text you've made.

Or write from two voices or points of view or time frames (before and after the eruption of Vesuvius, for example) or two of anything else you'd like to try.

Or write three.

When you have completed them, you might choose one, combine them, or toss both and go on to a new idea you came to while working on them.

Forcing a Metaphor

A **metaphor** is a comparison between "things" from different classes. These "things" can be objects, ideas, processes, or anything else we use language to represent. The metaphor can be expressed in a straightforward fashion: "You are the sunshine in my life." It can be streamlined into a name, often a product name: (Plymouth "Sundance." It can be done with a verb or verb phrase: "He was lucky to skate away from that disaster." Think of a **simile** as a metaphor that includes the word "like" or "as." Think of an **analogy** as a metaphor that has four parts: A is to B as C is to D. And don't worry about classifications. Worry about powerful, effective writing.

Metaphor is powerful because it is compact: "heart of stone." It involves the senses: "Don't rain on my parade." It explains one thing in terms of another: "Writing this paper is like wandering through a maze—I can't see where I'm going and I don't remember how I got here."

Some people use metaphor naturally. If you aren't one of them, you can still learn to write them. You can force a plant bulb to flower out of its normal season by changing the natural conditions—in effect, "fooling" the plant into blossoming in an unnatural season. In writing, you can force a metaphor into bloom by changing the natural conditions. Set out to write some, and you will. The following examples are one writer's attempts to explain an abstract process, his thinking. In "forcing" these metaphors, the student discovered something about his own thought processes and explained his discoveries in a way anyone can understand.

EXAMPLE 2.17 FORCING A METAPHOR

1. My thinking is like a bath tub filled to the top, with the water still running, because it is just about to overflow.
2. My thinking is like a pack rat's home because I never forget anything.
3. My thinking is like a fun house mirror, because what I am thinking comes out completely distorted when I speak.

—Bobby Bascomb

EXERCISE 2.17 FORCING A METAPHOR

Begin with the object or subject or topic you wish to write about. Let's say "your written voice" is the subject. You need to find five things with which to compare your voice. A "thing" can be an object, person, process, idea, or anything else with definable characteristics. Set up your paper to look like this:

My voice is/is like:

_____ *(thing 1)* because _____ .
_____ *(thing 2)* because _____ .
_____ *(thing 3)* because _____ .

When you select things for comparison, look for the unusual and the outrageous. The purpose of the metaphor is not to show what is already known, but to reveal a new way of looking at things. You should be as surprised at the discovery as any other reader.

To say your voice is "like a rasp because it's rough and raspy" is not very remarkable or new. Here's a simple rule to follow when listening to your writing for fresh language: If you've heard the phrase more than once or twice, it's probably a cliché.

After you've written five of these, drop the inessential words. Revise to make the verbs do the work. If you're determined to be raspy, "I rasp" is more forceful and direct than "my voice is like a rasp because it's raspy."

Strive for power and economy in the metaphors, and let the rest of the writing do the rest of the work. Select one or more of the metaphors and use them as a basis for further development.

Found Objects (or Pictures)

When you discover an interesting artifact, use it for a subject. If you are given a topic or subject, find an object or photograph or other visual associated with the subject and use it as a starting point.

A Found Object: Cleaning out the old garage, you discover an ancient scythe that belonged to a long-forgotten ancestor. Write about the man who wore the handle smooth with his callused hands. What did he think about as he cut a harvest swath through the field? Read a little. What is the handle called? What was used to sharpen the wicked curve of the blade?

Feel it. Go out and try to cut something with it. What muscles do you use? What does the motion feel like? What would it feel like after eight or ten hours in a field in the sun? Rest it on your shoulder. Lean on it at the end of the day. Go ahead and tell the story.

A Visual: You are assigned to write about "existentialism." You find some photographs and drawings of Sartre and Camus. You select the black and white photo of Camus looking into the camera. You start in one corner and describe everything you see in the photo, every little detail. Work your way across the photo in a generally diagonal path, gradually taking in all there is to see. You might try another writing with the same picture by taking a different path. Start in the middle and spiral outward, describing what you see when you take this path. You might describe the background and then move to the foreground.

In Example 2.18, you can reconstruct the path the writer took as she examined the found object.

EXAMPLE 2.18 FOUND OBJECTS

The object I found was a silver certificate $2 bill from 1976. I know that the United States government had made them, but I had never really seen one up close before. I found it wedged between the pages of a novel in the basement bookcase. The bill looks similar to the dollar bill, but with a few changes. The picture on the front was of President Jefferson. Along the outside edges there was a scrollwork pattern with the words "The United States of America" written on the bottom instead of the top. "In God we trust" was along the top above the president's face. It also had a green Department of the Treasury Seal over the word "two." It also had the signatures of the Department of Treasury and the Secretary of Treasury's at the bottom. On the left side was a seal that had what state the bill was printed in and what letter corresponds to that state. On the back of the bill, there is a zigzag pattern around the picture. The picture is of five delegates from the Continental Congress Signing the Declaration of Independence. On the bottom, there is a bannerlike scroll that denotes the value of the bill. On the top the words "United States of America." This represents what country and what value the bill offers.

—Gretchen Crouch

EXERCISE 2.18 FOUND OBJECTS OR VISUALS

Try this technique with the picture on the following page or with a picture or drawing of your own. In the middle of a sheet of opaque paper, cut a one-inch square. Place this over the picture and move it around until you find a focal point or interesting part of the picture. After you write about that square in some detail, uncover the picture and write about the relationship between that one-inch square and the rest of the picture. As an alternative to this activity, you can use one of the two methods described on page 60.

Getting Started on an Academic Task

These next six strategies begin with a form or way of thinking (for example, cause and effect) and apply that form to a topic. Studies of expository or nonfiction texts of various areas of study show the most common forms or thought structures represented in all of them. Table 2.2 presents them in order of occurrence.

TABLE 2.2 COMMON THOUGHT STRUCTURES IN NONFICTION

1. Defining
2. Giving the steps or directions of a process
3. Establishing a list, series, or order
4. Relating cause to effect, effect to cause
5. Comparing and contrasting
6. Solving problems

If these are the underlying "thinkings" in the writings of all content areas, then learning to use them will serve two purposes. First, you will think and *write* better in each area. Second, you will think and *read* better in each area.

Consider the courses you've taken so far. Make a mental list of the activities, lessons, problems, and other assignments you've had to complete. Wouldn't 75% of them fit into this list of categories:

1. Defining: "Tell what _____ means . . ."
2. Steps or directions: "Show how you would go about . . ."
3. List or series or order: "List the causes of _____ in order of _____ ."
4. Cause and effect: "Explain why _____ was a result of _____ ."
5. Comparing/contrasting: "Discuss the similarities/differences of _____ and _____ ."
6. Solving problems: "Given _____ (situation, numbers, variables, case), solve for _____ (*the* answer or *an* answer)."

If you can "do" these—in reading and writing and speaking and listening—you can *think* across the curriculum. But suppose you are in a course that has traditionally not used paper as part of its activities. What does this have to do with you? Are you going to write an essay before you can play football? Write a term paper on Benny Goodman before practicing the clarinet? Trace the history of the saw before cutting a stick of wood? The answer, in all cases, is "No." But you might draw up a game plan for your team in a particular sport—solving problems. You might explain how you're dealing with the difficulties in the clarinet part you're rehearsing—explaining a process. You might talk about the types of wood saws and what they're used for—comparing and contrasting.

Both in coaching and in competing in sports, it has been our experience that, as people practice, so they will play. Practice is important because it creates habits of body and mind that are required in order to play well and to continue improving. One purpose of the course you are taking is to create the habits of thought and expression required for playing well in the game of leaning. Writing for thinking asks you to "be aggressive out there" about your own learning.

The activities that follow can be used as they are or as models you can adapt to the particular question or topic you want to write about.

Defining

Defining is an attempt to say what something *is* or *means.* There is more than one way to define a subject or topic. Let's say you are defining "Topic A." You can give a synonym of A, classify A, tell how A is used, give important characteristics of A, trace the history of A, tell what A isn't, or give an outstanding example of A. Or you could do all of these, depending on your purpose. Remember that how you choose to define will determine what shows up in your definition.

Example 2.19 began as an opening move and resulted in a complete first draft. The topic the writer defined was "Myself."

EXAMPLE 2.19 DEFINING

Classify: When classifying myself I found that I was also stating what I am not and some of my key characteristics. I think of myself as a generally normal teenager whose life consists of school, family, friends and activities. I fit under the categories of junior, female, musician, thespian, student, and many others. In stating each of these there are descriptions and images to be painted.

Tell how it is used: The way I classify myself has a lot to do with how my life is "used." If I said that I was a nun, then I would be "used" in the proper religious context/manner, not as a model in a Jehovah witness pamphlet. Using words, titles and topics involves basic common sense and the abilities to sort out the taboo. I am used in a musical, drama, friendly, educationally, upper classman like way. I live my life in categories and there are subtle (subliminal) ground rules that go with each (found in the unpublished handbook of life) and so that is how I am "used."

Give key characteristics: I am considered a very complex, weird, indescribable person. I consider myself misunderstood, confused, but basically okay. I have been told that I really should take myself more seriously and not to batter myself so much. I don't like myself very much so, I am usually insulting and hard on myself, the usual-teenager-with-a-complex-syndrome. I am different than everyone else because I strive to be because I hate the clone-like monotony that surrounds me. For example, my hair is currently a shade of light burgundyish-purple (it was a very bad accident), but I do not have a nosering, a tattoo or wear combat, retro-sixties or leopard-print clothing. I fit stereotypes in a slight way, but then I diverge to myself. I play percussion—a loud and very physical, "manly" thing (I don't like stereotypes, but they seem to fit here), but then I am a violinist and a flutist, which are typically considered "delicate, like little song birds." I am me.

Give an outstanding example: An example of me is something that is hard for me to give. There are several of me: the school me, the with friends me, the with her parents me and then there's alone-in-my-head me. Since there's no one here to give a different example I will share what's going on in my head to show the real "me." I am thinking about writing and singing in my head to the music I am typing to. I am thinking that I am thinking that I am seriously going to hurt my family if they don't leave me alone and let me type like a madman. I am thinking about going to drama rehearsal and my lines that I am supposed to have memorized. I am thinking about how tired I am and how I'd *really* like to snooze, but can't because this is due. I am thinking about dinner because I am hungry. I am thinking if I think and then write down the wrong things they are going to send me away. Right now, obviously, is not a real good time to share.

Tell what it isn't: Well, right off the bat I am *not* an "it." I am not right now any of the following, give me few days, some sleep or caffeine and it will all change: mistaken, used, mistreated, tormented, sane, stable, awake, unhappy, bitter, happy, in pain, a bar dancer, racist, a liberalist, a voter, a driver, a clone, a snob, lonely, sad, excited, enthused, en-thralled, an excellent typist, a good speller, amused, giddy, depressed, overjoyed, sure, confused, comfortable or done. These are instant responses that change at the drop of a hat. You can't give yourself a rigid "not" classification because they are different every day.

Defining is what something is or means. From above you know a little of what I am, but I can't have a meaning. You can't look up Susan K. in the dictionary and find anything like this:

Susan (Soo':zen), noun. 5'6, chubby, purple haired and a funny nose. See Klemme, girl and Canajoharie High School for more on this topic.

I have a meaning in my own physical being and have life. I admit being only 16 doesn't sound like I've even had a chance to gain a meaning. You're probably right, but one day I hope to mean a lot to someone(s?) in the world and have purpose and meaning.

—Susan Klemme

EXERCISE 2.19 DEFINING

Identify your topic and write it on a piece of paper. From the list below, choose the types of definitions you want to write.

Topic: _____

Give a synonym:
Classify:
Tell how it is used:
Give key characteristics:
Give an outstanding example:
Trace the history of:
Tell what it *isn't:*

As quickly as you can, write the types of definitions you have selected. When you have finished, read what you've written and see which one (or how many) of these you'd like to use in a longer piece of writing. You might discover that you have the basis for an entire piece of writing about this topic. Think about different arrangements of the definitions you have written.

Steps or Directions for a Process

Writing about a process usually takes one of two forms: writing the steps you followed to do something, or writing the steps or directions you'd like someone else to follow. In either case, the order of steps is likely to be important. This technique is like a process memo, but a bit more formal. Example 2.20 tells the reader how to go about writing a goal.

EXAMPLE 2.20 STEPS OR DIRECTIONS FOR A PROCESS

Before writing about a goal that you would like to accomplish you need to write down a couple of goals that you would like to work on. Then you can look at each of them individually to see which one needs the most improvement, for you.

After you have found a particular goal, you should write down a few ideas about how you will go about working on it. When you have the activities planned out, go ahead and do them.

When you have done a few activities, ask yourself if it is working. If it is working you should prove to yourself that it has worked by writing down how you know. If you feel that it is not working, you may want to re-plan your activities and find an easier goal to work on for the moment until you can get used to the activities and the idea. If you don't want to try another goal, you may want to ask someone to help you accomplish your goal, because he or she may have some activities for you to follow.

—Amy Lemp

EXERCISE 2.20 STEPS OR DIRECTIONS FOR A PROCESS

Select an activity to write about and write a report of what you did, or directions for someone else to follow. Try writing the process for something you are an expert at, like tying shoelaces or eating spaghetti. *Note:* You may not need all the steps listed below. The writing you produce will be a process piece. You might wish to develop it into a longer process writing, or to use it as a part of another writing.

Activity or Process: _____

Brief description:

Step 1:

Step 2:

Step 3:

Step 4:

Step 5:

Step 6:

Establishing a List, Series, or Order

Establishing a list means arranging items in a useful order. The order may be based on size (largest to smallest), cost (least to most expensive), the alphabet (A to Z), time (earliest to latest), space (nearest to farthest), priority (most to least important), or some other characteristic. Note that each of these can be reversed, as well: Z to A order is still based on the alphabet, but in reverse. The point is that you choose a way of grouping things or classifying them.

Another form of classification is creating a hierarchy or taxonomy. Start with an area that interests you: sports cars. How do you group them (By color? Horsepower? Seating capacity? Make? Year? Cylinders? Turbocharged or not?) You then build your individuals into groups and the groups into larger groups until you have a sort of a tree diagram with all the specifics as the branches and twigs and the larger categories at the bottom. Example 2.21 shows three different ways to organize the same eight items.

EXAMPLE 2.21 ESTABLISHING A LIST, SERIES, OR ORDER

Items: Cross-country and Track Races: 3.1 miles, 2.8 miles, 2 miles, 1 mile, 800m, 400m, 200m, 100m

Items arranged in order: 3.1 miles, 2.8 miles, 1 mile, 800m, 2 miles, 400m, 200m, 100m

Reason for arrangement: My favorite race to my least favorite

Items in another order: 100m, 200m, 400m, 800m, 1 mile, 2 miles, 2.8 miles, 3.1 miles

Reason for arrangement: The shortest to longest

Items in another order: 100m, 200m, 400m, 800m, 2 miles, 1 mile, 2.8 miles, 3.1 miles

Reason for arrangement: My worst to my best race.

—Sarah Leonard

EXERCISE 2.21 ESTABLISHING A LIST, SERIES, OR ORDER

List (or find) the items to be arranged. On a piece of paper, list the items you start with, and then show your new arrangement, the order you establish. At the end, explain your reasons for the arrangement you chose. You may want to try two or three different arrangements.

Items:

Items arranged in an order:

Reason for this arrangement or order:

Items arranged in another order:

Reason for this order:

Tracing Cause and Effect

Cause-and-effect reasoning works in two directions. You might look at causes or conditions, and then predict what the future result will be. Weather reports predict results based on conditions or causes.

In addition to its use in making predictions, cause-and-effect thinking is also used to explain results. After an auto or airplane accident, investigators work backwards from the results and try to find the causes. Detective work involves the same kind of thinking.

An important feature of this type of thinking is the justification for linking the cause to the effect. It is not just a description of the process, but it gives the reasons for each step and the sequence of steps. Example 2.22 shows cause, effect, and linking.

EXAMPLE 2.22 TRACING CAUSE AND EFFECT

Cause: She loves horses.
Effect: She learned everything she could about them.
Link: She wanted to know everything because she loved them.

Cause: You want to start a report for English. You start writing with no firm plan in mind.
Effect: Several good ideas develop.
Link: You think and develop good ideas as you write.

—Sarah Leonard

EXERCISE 2.22 CAUSE AND EFFECT

Work out your cause-and-effect thinking by starting with cause and working toward effect, or the other way around. In either case, work out the missing part and show how you make the link.

Use your own notebook paper. After "Causes," write the condition(s) or cause(s). After "Effects," write the effect(s) or result(s). After "Link," explain how you link them—why you think the cause(s) would produce the effect(s).

Causes:

Effects:

Link:

Comparing and Contrasting

We're always comparing and contrasting—looking for similarities and differences. Our purposes can vary. We may need to choose one thing over another: "Which dessert should I order?" We may be arguing a point: "My car is better then yours." We may be trying to explain an unfamiliar thing by saying it is like a more familiar thing: "The transmission on the car works like the gear shift mechanism on your 10-speed." We may be seeking a creative insult: "Talking to you is like _____ ."

Example 2.23 shows you a comparison chart, complete with purpose statement and conclusion. The chart is designed to achieve the writer's purpose, to help her make some decisions about various types of colleges.

EXAMPLE 2.23 COMPARING AND CONTRASTING

Purpose

My purpose for choosing colleges to compare and contrast is to be able to help myself when it comes to this very important decision. In order to choose colleges one must know how to compare and contrast them in order to find a school that is suitable to a student. My purpose is to help me select the type of school that I will feel comfortable with financially, academically, in size, and in the type of school.

COLLEGES

	HUDSON VALLEY COMM. COLLEGE	SIENA	SUNY CORTLAND
Feature A Type of School	This is a 2-yr community college	This is a 4-yr private college	This is a 4-yr state college
Feature B Cost	$775/semester $1500 av. tuition	Tuition $5097/semester General cost $16,900/yr	Undergrad. $8923/yr in state Grad $10,125/yr in state (average)
Feature C Entrance Requirements	H.S. graduate Demonstrate adequate scholastic achievement (70-85 minimum average) Satisfactory completion of H.S. courses Satisfactory SAT or ACT	Application H.S. graduation transcript Recommendation CEEB results or ACT not req. Math 4 yrs Foreign lang	Application Transcript ACT or SAT scores; one recommendation and personal essay
Feature D Serves Biology Education	Provides courses for students who plan to transfer to a 4-yr college Secondary no educ. courses (yes)	Secondary education in biology	BA & BS SEC. ED.—BIO

Conclusion

This has helped me in determining what school best supports educational opportunities for me. A state 4-year or private 4-year is most suitable for my academic interests. But the financially reasonable way to go is a state school which is half the cost of the private school. The 2-year school is offering reasonable classes and is the easiest to get into and later transfer to a state or private school.

Comparing and contrasting has helped me review certain features of colleges that I am concerned with.

—Jen Ayers

EXERCISE 2.23 COMPARING AND CONTRASTING

Using the chart in Example 2.23 as a model, map out your comparison and contrast for two or three topics. Begin by stating your purpose: selecting, arguing, understanding, evaluating, etc. Next, fill in the names of your topics. These may be people, things, events, processes, ideas, or anything else you're studying.

Use your own notebook paper. Down the left-hand margin, fill in the names of features you're considering: size, cost, appeal, power, effectiveness, etc. Then complete the chart by writing on it what you know about each feature of each topic. Finish your work by drawing a conclusion, one related to your purpose, from your look at these topics.

Purpose:

Topic 1:

Topic 2:

Topic 3:

Feature A:

Feature B:

Feature C:

Feature D:

Conclusion (so what?):

Solving Problems

We can solve simple problems without even thinking about what we're doing or how we're doing it. Try this one:

2 + 3 = ?

Not hard. Now try this one:

What is the cube root of the number that is 2 less than the sum of half your weight plus your shoe size multiplied by 8?

Are you reaching for a pencil? As you can see, more complex or unfamiliar problems can best be approached with an organized method. Here is one such method to use:

1. Define the problem: State it in specific terms:

   "The back tire on my bike is flat."

2. Show the effects: Give the symptoms or results:

   "I can't ride to school, and I'll have to walk to school and then to practice."

3. Trace the causes: Identify the people, things, events, or other forces you think may have caused this:

   "There's a small nail stuck in the tire."

4. Hypothesize (suggest) a solution strategy: Tell what might be done to solve it:

   "I could remove the tire and put a patch on the tube."

5. Test your solution strategy: Try it or consider how well it might work:

   (You patch it and try to ride the bike.)

6. Evaluate the solution: How well does your solution work?:

   (The patch holds well, leaks slightly, or leaks terribly.)

7. If necessary, go back to step 3 or 4:

   If it leaks, you might patch again or replace the tube this time.

In Example 2.24, the writer uses this technique to work through a personal problem, getting along in her family. Besides illustrating the technique, the writer shows that not all problems are going to be solved in a page or so of writing.

EXAMPLE 2.24 SOLVING PROBLEMS

More complex or unfamiliar problems can be best approached with an organized method. I will attempt to use the given model to solve one of my recurring problems.

1. Define the problem: state it in specific terms:

My problem is my family and my relationship with them. I hate the things that happen with them that make me want to run away or kill them all.

2. Show the effects: give the symptoms or results:

Symptoms: my immense lack of self-confidence, my lack of a stable self-image and my great dislike of coming home.

3. Trace causes: identify the people, things, events, or other forces you think may have caused this:

My family in general, being the middle child and only girl, feeling resented by parents and them liking the other siblings better than me. My brother's birth when I was 10 was very hard on me because I had always been the baby and resented his presence. I had to constantly compete to receive attention, but eventually felt ignored. My older brother being perfect, the model "good" child, even up to this very day.

4. Hypothesize (suggest) a solution strategy: tell what might be done to solve it:

I have contemplated running away, killing them or just killing myself, but those are irrational and very immature ideas. My general plan is to go to college or the peace corps and forget that they are even alive. Then seek psychiatric help or receive heavy counseling sessions until I believe that I am cured of my complex.

5. Test your solution strategy: try it or consider how well it might work:

Since I have a while before graduation, I think I'll have to stick it out, calmly. I don't think I could forget them that easily and since they'd be paying for my college education I doubt I could completely ignore them. The peace corps involves a lot of shots and I have a fear of needles. Maybe the counseling and psychiatric help could come a little sooner.

6. Evaluate the solution: how well does your solution work:

I haven't tried because I am still sitting in front of this computer, but hopefully something good will become of this. (Ed McMahon will show up on my doorstep with a really big check with his picture on it!)

7. If necessary, go back to an earlier step:

I really don't want to and I am not going to. This exercise has shown that this model sticks strictly to writing problems and that everyday ones need people with leather couches in their offices to solve them.

—Susan Klemme

EXERCISE 2.24 SOLVING PROBLEMS

On your own paper, define the problem as you see it or as it is given to you. Then, complete the steps by writing a few specific sentences for each. *Note:* "Something must be done!" is *not* specific. Make sure that you tell who should do what, when and where, and why and how, if you can.

1.   Define the problem.
2.   Show the effects.
3.   Trace the causes.

4. Hypothesize a solution strategy.
5. Test the solution.
6. Evaluate the solution.
7. If necessary, go back to an earlier step.

A Word of Caution

No one of sound mind would try to use all of these techniques or even many of them for a single piece of writing. However, until you try some, you will not know which ones are most productive for you. If you have a chance, try various combinations of them for different types of writing. In a single month, you could experiment with each of them in your notebook.

Your literary writing, for example, might allow you to use openers that don't help you at all in the writing you do for other courses. The point is not to make every suggested technique work, but to find out what works for you, and to develop your own repertoire for writing. Remember that, at the end of this course of work, your portfolio will be more than a folder displaying your writings. It will also be what you know about, what you have learned to do, and what habits and practices you have developed. *You* will be your most important product.

COMPUTERS AT WORK:

Brainstorming with Your PC

Using a word processor for opening moves will help you to generate and manipulate text without the time and effort of recopying each version of your writing. When you discover what techniques work best for you—and you will probably develop some new ones of your own—you can make and store a file of templates or outlines on your word processing program. Then, for a new piece of writing, you can select from your personal menu of techniques the one or ones you want to begin.

Another way of brainstorming with a computer is to make a card file, using a database program or a hypertext program, in which to store ideas. You can make a computer file of books you have read and keep notes of parts you like and want to remember. You can also make a series of spaces around a topic that interests you. Suppose you are studying a Shakespearean play. You could make a file card for each of the following:

- Background of the Play
- History of Shakespeare, the Theater, and Later Productions including Films
- Class Responses to the Play
- Aspects of the Play: Plot, Character, Setting, Tone, Mood, Action, Images, and Metaphors

In each group of file cards you can include many categories of information.

Many writers keep their response journals or learning logs on a computer disk. They are able to retrieve ideas for papers. Keeping a separate disk or "folder" for each project enables you to have easy access and retrieval.

Chapter Summary

Accepting no excuses from yourself is a good way to get started. The opening moves are ways to "mine" the richness of knowledge and experience that you have, and ways to get beyond the superficial and automatic expressions that first come to mind. Some moves are explorations of topics, while others are based on certain kinds of thinking. Rather than master every technique, you need to find the ones that work for you and the kinds of writing you do. Using a word processor will help you to produce and manipulate the text generated in your opening moves.

Chapter Three will show you how to shape the writing you produce in opening moves to accomplish your purpose with your audience.

3 Giving Shape to Your Writing

Do You Know:

- Who your payoff audience is?
- How to identify an internal structure for your writing?
- Which structures to use for presenting facts, conclusions, or advice?
- How to set up your work with preview questions?

Looking Ahead

I n the last two chapters you discovered ways to find a direction and get started with audience and purpose. Now, you'll see how your payoff audience is connected to other audiences of your work. You'll also come to understand the difference between external logic, or form, and internal logic, the ways that thoughts are connected at various levels of purpose.

Most of this chapter is devoted to giving shape to your writing. Understanding the logical structure your work will take will help you to plan and to write. You will also see variations on a theme: a single topic treated in different ways by the same writer. Each "way" or style results in a different voice.

Audiences, Purposes, Forms

So, you've thought about audience and purpose and then used one or more of the opening moves described in Chapter 2 to write a few pages of text. Now what? What do you do next? How do you organize the writing? How do you select—from hundreds of forms—the best form for this work? And, then, how do you develop the work?

In Chapter 1, Table 1.1 showed five general purposes for writing, but form and purpose are not identical. Also, the purposes can overlap. You might write something beautiful to express yourself, but you also might be writing to convince your instructor that you know something about poetry. You might have different purposes for different audiences.

Imagine a baseball game. The batter scans the crowd, reads the sign from the base coach, smiles at his girlfriend, nods to the umpire, glares at the pitcher, gives a few practice swings, scratches, kicks, shrugs, and steps to the plate. How many audiences does he have for this prebatting performance? How many purposes? The batter might want to build suspense for the crowd, show the manager he pays attention to signs, and show his girlfriend, "This one's for you." In addition, the batter might want to get favorable calls from the umpire, terrorize the pitcher and throw off his concentration, and prepare himself to hit to improve his batting average. There may be even more purposes for audiences we don't even know about.

Similarly, even an apparently simple piece of writing can be complicated, even if it isn't as public a performance as being up to bat. Let's say you're asked to take the role of a character in a book you read and write a letter to another character—a letter about some interesting or mysterious point in the book that's never cleared up. In *The Great Gatsby*, for instance, Daisy gets a letter from Gatsby that is destroyed, the contents never revealed to the reader. Your assignment is to write the letter, which will then be read aloud to your peers.

How many audiences and purposes do you have? Since the letter is from Gatsby, Daisy is one audience (although she will never see your letter). Readers of *Gatsby* constitute another audience (they won't see it, either). You, of course, are your own audience. Your peers are another, and so is your instructor. Aren't there as many purposes as there are audiences for this letter?

In any writing situation, you need to distinguish between *ostensible* purposes and audiences, and *actual* purposes and audiences. The *payoff audience* is always one of the actual audiences. The **payoff audience** is the one that decides something about you on the basis of your writing:

- Your portfolio grade is "A";
- You are accepted at college "B";

- You can move on to level "C";
- You are a finalist in contest "D."

Your job, then, is to choose a form that allows you to accomplish the actual purpose through accomplishing the ostensible purpose. Remember, if the batter doesn't get a hit (or somehow get on base), none of the other purposes are accomplished, either. ("This strikeout's for you" doesn't have that nice ring to it, does it?) In the Gatsby letter example, whoever gives the grade is the payoff audience.

Even if there are no grades and there is no obvious payoff audience, there will still be some criteria for judging the usefulness or effectiveness or beauty or power or clarity of what you write. It's time to consider these criteria now.

Classifications: External and Internal Logic

Books about writing often classify kinds of writing into separate boxes. Unfortunately, just as purposes overlap, so do these categories. Think of the names of categories as points of focus; do not suffer over the "right" classification of each thing you write. Table 3.1 offers a convenient system for looking at writing, but not for deciding what to write or how to evaluate the writing.

TABLE 3.1 KINDS OF WRITING

	PURPOSE	**ISSUE**	**BUILDING BLOCKS**
NARRATIVE WRITING	Tells a story, real or imagined	What happened	Events
DESCRIPTIVE WRITING	Tells about appearance	What it looks like	Details (usually visual)
ANALYTIC WRITING	Tells how and why things work	Why it happened	Causes and effects
EXPOSITORY WRITING	Reveals something about a topic	What it is/is like	Explanations and classifications
ARGUMENTATIVE WRITING	Persuades the reader	What you should do/think	Various forms of appeals

Audiences and purposes are multiple; forms and classifications over-lap. What's more, forms can have differing internal and external logics. **External logic** refers to the outward form or shape of the communication. Some examples are a memo, a letter, a dialogue, or a poem. Internal logic refers to the flow of thought within that shape or form. If the external logic shows the shape of the document, the **internal logic** shows the shape of the thinking.

Let's look at one common internal logic, the *problem-solution pattern.* It usually begins with description of a problem and its effects, goes on to mention its causes, identifies a solution, and explains what good will result from solving the problem.

Letters of complaint typically use this internal logic. So do many Shakespearean and Petrarchan sonnets. And advertisements for painkill-ers, pimple creams, plant food, and political candidates. And the trouble-shooting guide for a snowblower, and the "Is He *Using* You?" article in the teen magazine, and the detective story, and the consultant's report on the collapse of the bridge. As a writer, you need to remember that the form is not the purpose. In fact, the *external* form or logic (the obituary, the business letter, the essay) is not the *internal* form or logic (problem-solution, statement-support, thesis-proof).

The next pages will show you some internal logics that are based not on the form you wish to write, but on the purpose you wish to accomplish. Following these explanations and examples will be preview questions to help you plan and look at your work with these internal logics. Next will come a research guide which shows you how to use these techniques to plan and complete research assignments in your courses. The chapter will end with examples of assignments you might encounter in different sub-ject areas.

Levels of Purpose: Fact, Conclusion, or Recommendation

Whenever we use speaking and writing to communicate, we rely on patterns and conventions. Reading from left to right, using paragraphs, punctuating ends of sentences, capitalizing certain letters—these are all conventions or agreements about language use that make communication easier for those who know "the rules of the road." In fact, a great part of traditional language instruction involves teaching these rules.

Other agreements or conventions are equally important, and go deeper than the surface or appearance of the communication. There are common patterns for organizing and reporting facts, conclusions, and recommen-dations. Let's consider some of these and the level of purpose each is best suited for.

Level One: Informational Writing

In Level One writing, the purpose is to give *information*—just the facts. Establishing a fact, for yourself or someone else, is the point. No conclusions need to be drawn by the writer, and no recommendations are made. Level One writings include textbooks, news articles, many nonfiction magazine articles, most reference works, and reports, papers, and letters.

Almost 85% of the reading we do in textbooks fits an informational pattern. This is not surprising, since textbooks usually present their views or classifications as if there could be no argument. Typical statements or topics found in textbooks might include the following:

There are three classes of rocks.

This problem can be solved with geometry, algebra, or constructions.

Most symphonies have four movements.

Continental U.S. has four time zones.

There are _____ types of common fasteners.

Three main exports of Chile are . . .

An effective player must be able to play offense and defense.

The three verb tenses are . . .

The four main food groups are . . .

As you can see, these pieces of informational writing usually present "the material" in the agreed-upon classification and categories of science, history, math, language, music, technology, health, or sports. Instructors don't often argue with accepted classifications or ways of organizing the material, and we don't often invite students to argue, either. Table 3.2 gives three patterns of organization typically used for Level One informational writings.

TABLE 3.2 PATTERNS OF ORGANIZATION:
               LEVEL ONE (INFORMATIONAL) WRITING

STATEMENT-SUPPORT

Statement: States a fact or facts

Support #1:   Gives details that support the statement

Support #2:   Gives more supporting details

Application: Tells how the information might be used

Example:

Statement: Common defenses in criminal cases include self-defense and insanity.

Support #1:   Self-defense is used when a threat to the defendant can be shown to have existed.

Support #2:   Insanity may be used in cases of special circumstances involving stress or upset.

Application: The circumstances of the crime can dictate the plea and the reasoning behind the plea.

TOPIC-ASPECT

Topic: Identifies an informational topic

Aspect #1:   Tells about one feature of the topic

Aspect #2:   Tells of another feature

Application: Tells how the information might be used

Example:

Topic: Rome has many tourist attractions.

Aspect #1:   Vatican City appeals to many.

Aspect #2:   In Ancient Rome, the Coliseum is worth the trip.

Application: If you ever visit Rome, you'll have plenty to see.

NEWS

Lead paragraph: Tells who, what, where, when, why, and how in brief

Next paragraph: Expands these facts in more detail

Next paragraph: Adds further detail

More paragraphs: Add further detail

Example:

Lead Paragraph: Early Friday morning, a bomb discovered in the parking lot of Sangertown Mall was removed by authorities and safely detonated with no damage or injury.

Next Paragraph: A shopper, noticing a bag on the pavement, went to retrieve it and saw wires and other mechanisms inside. Police were summoned, who then called the bomb squad from Albany. A robot placed the device in a safe container and transported it into the woods south of the mall, where it was safely detonated.

Next Paragraph: The bomb, consisting of three gallons of gasoline and a detonator, was rigged to explode if it was tampered with. Detectives from the Utica Police Department are continuing the investigation.

Note: News articles generally appear with headlines that further condense the lead paragraph into a few words.

EXERCISE 3.1 INFORMATIONAL WRITING

Try to complete three pieces of writing (or outlines) in the informational pattern. You can start with writings you completed in response to the "Opening Moves" exercises in Chapter 2, or just start from scratch. You may want to look back at the examples in Table 3.2.

Use the outlines that follow as guides for the shape of your writing. Each part may be a sentence, a paragraph, a series of paragraphs, or an entire chapter of a book. For this activity, aim for one paragraph per pattern part. Use as many supports, aspects, or other features as you need to develop your topic. Remember that the main purpose of this type of writing is to give information about a topic.

Statement-Support
Statement:
Support #1:
Support #2:
Application:

Topic-Aspect
Topic:
Aspect #1:
Aspect #2:
Application:

News
Lead Paragraph:
Next Paragraph:
Next Paragraph:
More Paragraphs:

Level Two: Interpretive and Analytical Writing

Level Two writings go beyond presenting facts. They draw conclusions or interpret meanings from these facts or statistics. If a Level One report showed that participation in athletics was down 8%, a Level Two essay might suggest why that has happened.

Level Two writings make assertions that are *not* necessarily common agreements, and so there is a burden of proof for these assertions. These writings attempt to determine meaning, blame, or cause, and so they require evidence. Level Two writings include scientific and technical journal articles, laboratory reports, analyses, critical reports and papers, projections of future events or outcomes, and planning sheets and flowcharts.

Thesis-proof organization (Table 3.3) can be used for the many types of documents at Level Two. This pattern, an old workhorse of expository writing courses, is perhaps the one most universally taught in composition courses in school and college. A thesis differs from a statement in that a **thesis** is by definition an arguable assertion. It has a subject and a predicate, both of which have to be defined and explained. It is understood that there are other assertions that could be made about the same topic.

TABLE 3.3 PATTERN OF ORGANIZATION:
LEVEL TWO (INTERPRETIVE AND ANALYTICAL) WRITING

<table>
<tr><td colspan="2" align="center">**THESIS-PROOF**</td></tr>
<tr><td>**Thesis:**</td><td>States a conclusion or interpretation that will be proven</td></tr>
<tr><td>**Proof #1:**</td><td>Gives evidence to prove this thesis</td></tr>
<tr><td>**Proof #2:**</td><td>Gives further evidence as proof</td></tr>
<tr><td>**Significance:**</td><td>Suggests the consequences or implications (if the thesis can be proven, then what might we expect to follow?)</td></tr>
<tr><td>*Example:*</td><td></td></tr>
<tr><td>**Thesis:**</td><td>Democratic capitalism [*the subject of which must be defined*] is becoming the dominant political economic system in the world [*the predicate of which will be proved*].</td></tr>
<tr><td>**Proof #1:**</td><td>The breakup of the Soviet Union has pushed former satellites toward democratic and capitalistic systems.</td></tr>
<tr><td>**Proof #2:**</td><td>China, the last bastion of communism, is also moving toward free markets and private ownership.</td></tr>
<tr><td>**Significance:**</td><td>We can expect the market of the future to be composed of variations on the theme of the free-market economy.</td></tr>
</table>

EXERCISE 3.2 INTERPRETIVE AND ANALYTICAL WRITING

Complete a piece of writing (or outline) in the thesis-proof pattern. You can start with a writing you completed in response to the "Opening Moves" exercises in Chapter 2, or just start from scratch. You may want to look back at the examples in Table 3.3.

Use the outline that follows as a guide for the shape of your writing. Each part may be a sentence, a paragraph, a series of paragraphs, or an entire chapter of a book. For this activity, aim for one paragraph per pattern part. Use as many proofs as you need to develop your topic. Remember that the main purpose of this type of writing is to draw a conclusion or make an interpretation.

Thesis-Proof

Thesis:

Proof #1:

Proof #2:

Significance:

Level Three: Persuasive Writing

Level Three writings go beyond facts and beyond interpretations of facts. Level Three writings give advice or recommendations. Here is a quick way to look at the relationship among the three levels: Level One asks, "What happened?" Level Two asks, "Why? How? So what?" Level Three asks, "What should we do about it?"

Level Three writings may be based on facts and interpretations, but their purpose is to persuade the reader (or listener) to think in a certain way, to buy a certain thing, to vote in a certain way, or to act in a particular way (Table 3.4). There is always a "bottom line" in Level Three writings, and the bottom line is a call to action: "Do _____." Level Three writings include editorials, position papers, advisory reports and papers, evaluations and recommendations, reviews, letters of complaint, advertisements, solution strategies, and troubleshooting guides.

TABLE 3.4 PATTERNS OF ORGANIZATION: LEVEL THREE (PERSUASIVE) WRITING

OPINION-REASON	
Opinion:	States an opinion, an arguable interpretation or view
Reason #1:	Gives evidence to support this opinion
Reason #2:	Gives further evidence
Recommendation:	Recommends a particular course of action
Example:	
Opinion:	Scientific research must focus on the two areas of health and the environment.
Reason #1:	Healthy people in a healthful environment is the ultimate goal of science and technology.
Reason #2:	Space exploration, weapons development, and other areas of research are less important and must be subordinated.
Recommendation:	Research grants based on federal monies should be restricted to these two critical areas.

PROBLEM-SOLUTION

Problem: Defines a problem

Effects: Gives the symptoms or results of this problem

Causes: Suggests the causes of the problem

Solution: Recommends a solution strategy

Significance: Tells the benefits the solution could bring

Example (a progress report):

Problem: Although he could do well in _____ , Clyde is not passing the course at present.

Effects: Unless there is a dramatic change, he will fail this course and have to repeat it next year.

Causes: He is absent from school at least two days each week, and he can never get caught up with the rest of the class.

Solution: Make sure he comes to school every day—not just for the rest of the quarter, but for the rest of the year.

Significance: With regular attendance, he should be able to complete the work and pass the course.

EXERCISE 3.3 PERSUASIVE WRITING

Try to complete two pieces of writing (or outlines) in the persuasive patterns. You can start with writings you completed in response to the "Opening Moves" exercises in Chapter 2, or just start from scratch. You may want to look back at the examples in Table 3.4.

Use the outlines that follow as guides for the shape of your writing. Each part may be a sentence, a paragraph, a series of paragraphs, or an entire chapter of a book. For this activity, aim for one paragraph per pattern part. Use as many causes, effects, reasons, or other features as you need to develop your topic. Remember that the "bottom line" of persuasive writing is to convince someone to think or act in a certain way.

Opinion-Reason
Opinion:
Reason #1:
Reason #2:
Recommendation:

Problem-Solution
Problem:
Effects:
Causes:
Solution:
Significance:

Note that such an organizing scheme determines the internal logic of a document, but not its size. For example, you can write a Problem-Solution paragraph or write a 20-page paper in that same pattern. Also, there is no "correct" number of supports or proofs or reasons. A test question or assignment may ask for a particular number ("Support your opinion with two reasons . . ."), or the number may be dictated by the scope of the assignment, the materials available, and other factors.

Relating Internal Logic to Purpose

When you receive an assignment or have to develop a topic into an assignment for a report or paper, you can try an internal logic scheme that is related to the purpose you identify for the research and writing. Understanding the logical structure the paper will take is a big help in planning and conducting the necessary research.

Most of your academic writing—writing you are assigned to do for a course—will be *work for hire.* You need to produce something that has shape and movement recognizable to the person who "hired" you. In most cases, if you're hired to design an obelisk, don't hand in sketches for an outhouse, even if it could be built with the same number of stones.

Table 3.5 shows another way of classifying the forms of your writing. Your instructor may give you yet another system.

TABLE 3.5 TYPICAL ORGANIZATIONS OF DISCOURSE

ORGANIZED BY TIME

1. *Narration:* Chronological development. May be rearranged with flashbacks or may have two or more simultaneous series of events.
2. *Process:* Chronological or step-by-step development. May include a list of parts or ingredients.

Typical Signals:

once   first   second   later   and   next   after   before   then

3. *Cause-effect:* Like process, but may go from effect to cause or from cause to effect.

Typical Signals:

the reason for   consequently   therefore   by means of   thus
result from   and so   because   effect

ORGANIZED BY SPACE

1. *Descriptive:* Develops by a geometrical or geographical arrangement—usually horizontal, vertical, or circular. May follow a map or a topographical arrangement.

Typical Signals:

besides   below   down from   as we move around   above   in front of
near   as you go about   next to   behind   following   preceding

ORGANIZED BY COMMON LOGIC

1. *Classificatory:* Develops by dividing object or event into parts and explaining relationships or difference of parts.
2. *Definitive:* Develops by giving distinctions of the object or event from others similar to it.

Typical Signals:

to constitute   to limit   to let us define   may be divided   progressive succession
as follows   into   is called   is seen   is made up of

3. *Comparison-contrast:* Organized by relating or differentiating two or more objects or events.

Typical Signals:

may be distinguished from   compared to   as   but   differs from
distinct from   on the other hand

4. *Pros and Cons:* Organized by showing strengths and weaknesses (put the one you want to emphasize last)

Typical Signals

strongly support   against   in fact fail to   indeed do not consider   truly deny
unquestionable   fail to support

Which format should you use? In an academic or business assignment, use the form that is most familiar to and recognizable by the audience. What is your audience expecting? Should you give it to them or surprise them? For other writing, use the form that makes most sense to you.

In different situations, different features of the work may become important. If your teacher likes long papers, write long ones. If your boss likes short memos, keep them short. If your mother likes to laugh, make it funny. If your prospective employers like "approved" resumé format, then use what they prefer. If your master's degree requires you to write a practicum, then use the problem-solution organization.

Setting Up the Work

When you don't feel like surprising the reader, you can anticipate the shape the reader expects for the writing and plan for your work to come out that way. (It still might not come out that way, but you can plan . . .)

Let's call this *setting up the work:* seeing the shape your work might take before you write very much of it. This preliminary work can be every bit as powerful for you as revising, and twice as efficient. When shape is important, it is much easier to preorganize than to reorganize.

Take this book, for example. We wrote a prospectus, a general content outline, before the three of us started working on it. Within various chapters, some things have changed, but the purpose, the content, and the order of chapters has changed very little.

Checklists 3.1 through 3.6 which follow give you preview questions to help you with your writing. First, they can be used to outline or draft an early version of a piece. Next, you can use the questions to see that your outline or draft fulfills the requirements of the scheme of internal logic you've chosen. Using these questions as lenses through which to see your writing might also help you to decide if you've chosen an effective scheme of internal logic to accomplish your purpose. Finally, the checklists can help you consider the important elements of your writing before you go to a final draft.

The first task, remember, is to determine from the assignment what kind of structure your particular task seems to call for. Then, use the appropriate checklist to help you deal with your plans for responding to it. These plans will get you on the way. Even if you have a sudden inspiration halfway through the paper that causes you to redraw your plans, you can use the checklist to help you revise your plans and make sure you are responding to the problem.

CHECKLIST 3.1 NEWS ORGANIZATION—PREVIEW QUESTIONS

Lead
- What should the first sentence be? Which of the six news questions should it try to answer?
- What are your readers likely to already know about this topic or event?

Next Paragraph
- What is the most important part of the story to detail?
- How should you explain it?
- What details or subtopics should be included?

Next Paragraph
- What part of the story should be detailed next?
- How will you link it with the previous paragraph?
- What details or subtopics should be included?

Next Paragraph
- What part of the story should be detailed next?
- How will you link it with previous paragraphs?
- What details or subtopics should be included?

Last Paragraph
- What part of the story should be detailed last to wrap it up?
- How will you link it to previous paragraphs?
- What details or subtopics should be included?
- How can you end the article with a satisfying close?
- What should the last sentence be?

CHECKLIST 3.2 TOPIC-ASPECT ORGANIZATION—PREVIEW QUESTIONS

Topic
- How will you define this topic and give it shape? What features or aspects of this topic will you select and point out to your audience?

- How much is your audience likely to know about this topic? Will your treatment of the topic be detailed or general?
- What method of development should you use for this first pattern part? Should you make a list? Give a description? Analyze?
- Where should you place the topic sentence for this pattern part?

Aspect 1

- Of the aspects you will discuss, which should come first? Should you begin with the most interesting or important feature, or build up to it?
- How will you link this aspect to the topic and the aspects that follow? What method of development will you use here?
- If you use this method of development, where should you place the topic sentence for this pattern part?

Aspect 2

- What is the next aspect or feature you will present to your audience? How can you link it to the aspects that come before and after it?
- What method of development can you use for this aspect? If you use this method of development, where should you put the topic sentence for this pattern part?

Aspect 3

- What is the final feature or aspect of this topic? How does this aspect complete your treatment of the topic?
- What method of development should you use for this final aspect?
- Using this method of development, where should you place the topic sentence for this final aspect?

Application

- How can your audience use the information you've given about this topic? Can you relate this topic to other topics of importance or interest? Can you relate the topic to the day-to-day experience of your audience?
- How will you sum up the aspects of this topic in the application? What method of development will you use?
- Where should you place the topic sentence for this final pattern part?

CHECKLIST 3.3 STATEMENT-SUPPORT ORGANIZATION—
PREVIEW QUESTIONS

Statement

- What is the central statement or main point of this writing?
- How much does your audience already know about this topic? Given your purpose, how heavy should you make the information load?
- What kinds of support will be most interesting and useful to your audience?
- To make this statement to your audience, what method of development would be most effective?
- Where should you place the topic sentence?

Support 1

- Which one of your supports should come first? How will you link this first support to the statement?
- What method of development should you use for this support?
- If you use this method, where should you place the topic sentence?

Support 2

- What is the next support or feature of interest or importance to your audience? How will you relate it to the supports that come before and after it?
- What would be an effective method of development for this pattern part?
- Where should you place the topic sentence?

Support 3

- If you have more than three supports, group the rest of them here. You can deal with them separately when you write the first draft.
- What is the final support for your statement? How will you link it to the other supports? To the application which follows?
- What method of development will you use for this final support?
- Where should you place the topic sentence?

Application

- How can your audience use the information you've given? Can you relate this to other topics of interest or importance? to the day-to-day experience of your audience?

- How will you sum up your statement and supports in this application? What method of development will you use?
- Where should you place the topic sentence for this final pattern part? How can you make an effective closing? What should the last sentence be?

CHECKLIST 3.4 THESIS-PROOF ORGANIZATION—PREVIEW QUESTIONS

Thesis

- What is the thesis or main point you are setting out to prove? What does your audience already know about this issue? Are they likely to agree with your thesis, or will you be arguing against prevailing views?
- What kinds of evidence will be most convincing to your audience?
- To present this thesis to your audience, what method of development will be most effective? Should you use analogy, deductive reasoning, or analysis?
- If you use this method of development, where should you place the topic sentence for this pattern part?

Proof 1

- Which proof or evidence should you present first? Should you start with the strongest proof or build up to it? How will you relate this proof to your thesis? To the later proofs?
- What method of development should you use for this first proof?
- Where should you place the topic sentence for this pattern part?

Proof 2

- What should be the next proof? How will you link this proof to your thesis? How will you link this proof with the proof or proofs before and after it?
- What method of development would be appropriate for this second proof?
- If you use this method of development, where should you put the topic sentence for this pattern part?

Proof 3

- If you have more than three proofs, group the rest here. You can separate them when you retrieve the file with your word processing program.
- What should be the final proof or culminating evidence? How does this proof complete your argument? What is the progression of your proof?
- How will you relate this proof to the earlier proofs and to the significance? What method of development will be effective for this final proof?
- If you use this method of development, where should you place the topic sentence for this pattern part?

Significance

- If the audience accepts your thesis and proof, what are the implications? What do you want the reader to conclude or to see as significant? How many parts are there to this significance?
- How will you show your audience the meaning of the thesis— the effects or results they can expect?
- How will you relate this significance or meaning to the thesis and proofs? What method of development will be effective for this significance?
- If you use this method of development, where should you place the final topic sentence for this writing?

CHECKLIST 3.5 OPINION-REASON ORGANIZATION—
PREVIEW QUESTIONS

Opinion

- How much does your audience already know about this controversial issue? Are they likely to agree with you, or will you be arguing against prevailing opinion? What details will be most convincing to present to this audience?
- To present this opinion or view to your audience, what method of development would be most effective? Should you build an image, tell a story, give a description?
- If you use this method of development, where should you place the topic sentence for this pattern part?

Reason 1

- In a writing of this size, how many reasons should you include: all you can think of, or a few of the most important ones? Which one should be presented first? Should you start with the most important or build up to it?
- What method of development would be useful in presenting this first reason? How can you relate this reason to your opinion?
- With this method of development, where should you place the topic sentence for this pattern part?

Reason 2

- What is the second main reason for agreeing with your opinion? What evidence can you give to link this reason to your opinion? To the reason or reasons that come before and after it? To the recommendation?
- What method of development should you use for this pattern part?
- If you use this method of development, where should you put the topic sentence for this pattern part?

Reason 3

- If you have more than three reasons, group the rest here. You can separate them when you retrieve the file with your word processing program.
- How does this final reason complete your argument? How will you relate it to your earlier reasons and to the recommendation?
- What method of development should you use for this final reason?
- Using this method of development, where should you place the topic sentence for this pattern part?

Recommendation

- What do you want the reader to think or do? Whose effort is needed? In what ways? What resources—money, time, and people—are required?
- What are the benefits of following your recommendation? How many benefits are there? What kinds? For which individuals and groups? Can you show how these benefits will be seen?
- What method of development can you use to illustrate the workings and benefits of your recommendation? Would comparing and contrasting give a "before-and-after" picture?
- If you use this method of development, where should you place the topic sentence for this pattern part?

CHECKLIST 3.6 PROBLEM-SOLUTION ORGANIZATION—
PREVIEW QUESTIONS

Problem

- How much does your audience already know about this problem?
- Would they even agree with you that there is a problem?
- What details will be convincing to present to this audience?
- What method of development would be most effective? Should you tell a story, build an image, make a comparison, give a description?
- With this method of development, where should you put the topic sentence?

Effects

- What are the most important effects of this problem?
- Should you focus on a few or list many of them?
- How can you show that these effects are important to your audience—how they will be affected?
- Can you relate these effects directly to the problem? To the causes?

Causes

- How many causes will you present? Do you have to rule out other causes to isolate the ones you'll deal with?
- What evidence do you have to establish these causes for your audience?
- Can you directly relate the causes to the effects? To the solution you will propose?
- What method of development will best present the causes?

Solution

- How many solutions will you propose? Do you need to show why other possible solutions won't work as well as yours?
- How can you give enough detail to show how your solution will work?
- Does your solution directly address the causes you identify?

Significance

- What are all the benefits of your solution strategy—both immediate benefits and long-range ones?

- In what specific ways will different groups—especially those in the audience—benefit? Can you illustrate the benefits?
- How can you bring the paper to a solid close? What should your last paragraph be?

Choosing Your Voice

Everything that we have said in this chapter leads up to some rather simple advice: *Think of your audience and purpose each time you write.* We have said it a number of different ways. We might even go at it another way. You have a choice of how you present yourself in your writing. In fact, you have a number of choices; which one you make is up to you and your sense of what you want to do with this piece of writing for this purpose and this audience. In the following pages, we present a set of examples of choices that most writers face: whether to focus on one aspect of the topic or several; whether to be abstract or concrete, whether to use figurative or literal language, whether to approach the topic with personal references or whether to be impersonal; whether to organize the paragraphs with clear logical signals or whether to use an organization that flows like a set of reflections and thoughts; and whether to treat the topic seriously or humorously. Let's say your task is to write a composition about your community. The examples that follow show some of the choices you might make.

Telling Everything vs. Focusing on One Aspect

Tell Everything

1. My community has a shortage of housing
   a. There are many families crowded into buildings that are too small
   b. The community should build more housing
2. The streets and buildings are not repaired
   a. Every street has potholes
   b. The public buildings have peeling paint
   c. The community should make repairs
3. The schools are located away from where people live
   a. As the community has grown the schools have not moved with the new housing

b. The schools should be moved or there should be better busing
4. There is little for young people to do
   a. There are few jobs for people after they graduate from school
   b. There are no business opportunities
   c. People usually move away
   d. The community should attract new business

Focus on One Thesis

1. As my community has grown in size, it has not promoted enough opportunity for work
   a. There is only one factory in town
   b. There are a few shops and no malls
   c. Young people can only work for their families or move out
   d. As a result young people leave the community
2. The community should attract more industry and business opportunity
   a. The community should encourage new industry
   b. There is sufficient population to develop a shopping mall
   c. The community should provide job training for young people
   d. These features would encourage young people to stay

Which do you prefer? Which do you think will make a better impact on the audience that you are trying to reach?

Keeping It Abstract vs. Making It Concrete

Should you put a lot of details into your paragraphs? Will too many details make people lose the point?

Keep It Abstract

The most serious problem in my community is that people do not care for the appearance of the buildings or the environment. It seems that both the individual citizens and the local government consider other things to be more important than making the community an attractive place to live. Buildings that are older are allowed to deteriorate, and when new buildings are erected, the signs of construction may remain for long periods after the work is finished. This lack of care can be seen in the streets and the various public places around the community. The problem does not appear to be one of a lack of money but a lack of interest.

Use Many Details

The most serious problem in my community is the ugliness and mess which makes the community an unattractive place to live. A person can walk down any street and see houses with broken windows or with junk piled around them. Often the grass isn't even cut. In the main part of town, the old public buildings are dirty and the paint is peeling from the walls. The new town garage was finished a year ago and it is being used, but the piles of lumber for construction are still sitting there and the dirt is still piled up from where the bulldozer did the excavation. There is not a street that doesn't have a pothole that needs to be filled; the benches in the town park are mostly broken, and the plumbing in the park lavatory hasn't worked for a year. The community is rich enough; they buy new trucks and cars for the mayor. The police get new squad cars and new uniforms. They are even building a new firehouse, and there is another park planned.

Both of these paragraphs are well organized; which do you think would fit into your paper better? How much of the detail depends on whether the readers live in the community or not?

Using Figurative vs. Literal Language

Another stylistic question is how literal or figurative you should be. Will your audience react better to language that is rich in metaphors and sensuous imagery, or do they prefer "plain talk"?

Use Figurative Language

The bluebird flits from one dry perch to another nervously. Butterflies search for budded sweet nectar blossoms while the young bear, thick-coated, paces his cage. North to south paces, over and over, watched intently by the old mother bear. Nearby the peacock, tail spread, beady-eyed. My best friend, Kara, wanting so much to flee. She darts from here to there to me—looking for escape, a reason to fly from this place. Who can blame her? Who cannot understand her need? Hope, growth, life are impossible. The poison in the air pervades all—places, people, things. She suffocates, she gasps for breath, she droops. And my community? I weep. Where are the sweet smelling blossoms and the clear tinkling bells from the high parts? The insistent drone of work whistles hypnotize, and the moan of the wheels blot the song. The press of gray brown despair tortures the souls of the bluebirds. Peacocks droop as the poison works, enveloping and endangering and ending. I must run to the blossoms and bells tinkling. The wheels crush the spirit, and helpless, tortured, cries drown the open song. Spew out the poison, my community, and open the cage doors.

Use Plain Language

My friend Misa feels as I do that our community offers no opportunity for us and our friends. We often talk to each other and discuss the arguments and reasons we will present to our families for leaving here. There are no jobs for us here. No future is possible here except to join the crowds of other people, young and old, who are hungry and listless. The old factory whistle sounds at the same time every day, signaling old, tired, bored workers to produce the exported goods. The work days are long, the money is little but the boredom is great for those fortunate enough to have a job. The officials accept the situation here as inevitable and fixed. Life goes on as it always has with no changes except declines in the quality of life. Opportunities are lacking for young people in all areas, personal, social, economic and political. The youth are doomed here to a life worse than their mother and fathers had. The community has no plans and goals for the future, no leaders to guide. The problems are great.

This choice is not an easy one. The figurative writing style asks the reader to consider the way you are writing and to pay attention to you as a writer. The plain style tends to focus the reader's attention more on the topic.

Determining the Level of Formality

The next choice is like the last one; it makes you decide whether you want the reader (a) to be aware of you, the writer, as a person who has feelings and thoughts about the subject, or (b) to be focused on the subject alone, with you, the writer, functioning as a distant authority. This was a choice that we had to make in the writing of this textbook.

Be Personal

In order to describe the main problem in my community, I shall tell you about my family. I live at home with my mother and father and an older brother. I have two older sisters but they have left home and gone to the city—one to work as a secretary, the other to work in a bank. My older brother is about to leave also. You see, my father is foreman in the factory and my mother works at home taking care of the family and the small garden. The factory is the only place where there are jobs unless one wants to be a farmer or unless you happen to own one of the shops. My uncle owns a shop and his children work for him, so there are no jobs for others. The factory is not very big and the work is dull. If a person wants to improve, the way my sisters and brothers do, a person has to leave. I really like this town, and I have many friends here, but I also want to do something different. I suppose I will move away when I finish school.

Be Impersonal

The major problem of the community is a lack of opportunity for young people. The community has three shops: a grocery, a small clothing shop, and a small hardware and tool shop, as well as a branch of the bank. There is also a small factory that employs about seventy-five people. Apart from that, the only other work that people do in the community is farm work and teaching in the school. There are more young people than there are jobs, and many of the jobs are boring, particularly if people want to get ahead in the world. Some of the young people are content to work in the factory or for their parents in a shop or on the farms. Only a few, however, want to teach in the school. As a result of this situation, about half of the young people who finish school leave the community.

Again the choice is not an easy one, and it depends on what sort of a relationship you want to establish with your audience.

Determining Style

Although it may seem a bit strange to you, one choice you have is whether to make your paragraphs appear to be logical by using the kinds of connectives between sentences that show various relationships or to make the writing appear as it is following your mind. This latter style relies on signals of the thought process, particularly repetitions of images, words, and phrases rather than connective words (we will cover this more in the grammar and style appendix.

Be Logical

One of the first things the leaders in my community could do to make the community more attractive is to create a campaign to make the houses more attractive. If the leaders were to award prizes for the family that did the best job of fixing its house and cleaning the surrounding grounds, most families would accept the challenge. After first giving awards to families, the community could then expand the plan to public buildings and parks. Prizes and awards could go to groups of volunteers who would undertake the work of fixing these places and making them pretty. One might argue that these volunteers would not want to pay money for materials such as tools and paint. The cost to an individual or a group would, therefore, only be the cost of time. If everyone were to join, moreover, the amount of time would not be too great for any one person. By following a process of individual awards to group awards, the leaders could help make my community attractive.

Show Your Thought Process

The leaders of the community could make the place more attractive by helping people fix up and clean up their own houses and community buildings. I mean that people probably just need a start. Imagine what would happen if the leaders gave prizes to the people who help the most. One prize might go to the neatest garden area. Then another prize might go to the prettiest house. It would not be for the original design, but for the best cleaning, fixing, and painting. Then, other people could win an award for picking up the rubbish in town square. It is usually filthy, with trash in the bushes. The town leaders could give out paint and tools to help, by the way. They could lend them to people to work on their own homes on days when the town workers do not need them. At the end, it would be nice to see banners and flags above the streets. The whole community would be bright and shiny. You would agree it would be a pleasant place to live, and the leaders and the people would have common goals and a sense of pride.

The second paragraph is similar to the style of many popular magazines; the first one is more like that of formal papers. Again the choice says something about how you appear to your audience, relaxed or all dressed up.

Tone and Attitude

The final choice is just how serious you should be. A lot of people don't appreciate humor in writing about a serious subject; but some find that they will accept a serious message better if there are a few jokes thrown in.

Be Serious

There are a number of problems in my community but most of them would take a lot of time and money to solve. There is, however, one problem which is an acute one but which could be resolved without spending large sums of money. That is the problem of boredom. Nothing exciting ever seems to happen in the community. Yet, this need not have to be so. With some creative ideas and community spirit a lot could be done. The mayor could set up a committee consisting of both older and younger people to recommend new activities. These might include choirs for children and for adults, and perhaps an amateur orchestra or band and an amateur theater group. There might be challenge matches or games between blocks or districts. People might revive old handicraft skills and show how different things were done in the past and what the things looked like. People might help to lay out a jogging track in a park or in a forest. These are only a few examples of what might be done to resist the boredom of inactivity. Different kinds of solutions would have to be devised to suit local circumstances.

Be Playful or Humorous

Any problems in my community? Are you kidding? There are nothing but problems. We have so many problems that we could easily organize a sale and sell a lot at a bargain and still have more than enough for home consumption. The greatest problem is boredom. Griping about problems never did any good, however. What we need is a lot of action backed with a pinch of thinking. We have to be careful with thinking though. It might develop like a habit and nothing good ever came from too much thinking. Never fear. These are some ideas produced with very little thought. The mayor might set up a committee consisting of the greatest bores in town. They would never be able to finish their work and we would never hear from them again. That alone would go a long way to improve local conversation. Those with no need for music but with a great desire for performing in public might be asked to form a choir or a band to be led by a very exacting musician. They would spend all their time practicing and torturing each other but not the rest of us. Other bores might be encouraged to take up football or skiing. Soon most of them would be lying in hospital with broken legs. Several weeks of relief! These are only a few examples of what might be done to combat boredom in the community. Different kinds of solutions would have to be devised to cope with the local variety of bores.

EXERCISE 3.4 CHOOSING YOUR VOICE

Start this exercise by selecting six responses you have written from the "Opening Moves" section in Chapter 2 or from Exercises 3.1–3.3 from this chapter. For each piece of writing, choose one of the variables below and rewrite (or expand) your earlier draft in two versions: one at each extreme of the variable.

For example, let's say you wrote (for Exercise 3.1) a news story about a recent event. You might choose the variable of "Focus" below and write two versions of the story, one that tells everything, and another that highlights one aspect of the story. If you wrote 20 opening lines for a story (see Exercise 2.14), you might choose "Tone" and write two drafts of the story, one serious and the other humorous and light.

Read each earlier piece and imagine two different audiences and two different purposes for the writing. With audience and purpose in mind, choices about language and style and tone are easier to make. You do not have to produce finished writings in this exercise. If you write for twenty minutes for each variable, you will get the "flavor" of each extreme. Match up the variables with the six pieces you want to develop, and write two extremes for each.

Variable	┌─────── Two Extremes ───────┐	
Focus	Tell everything	Focus on one aspect
Concreteness	Keep it abstract	Make it concrete
Language	Use figurative language	Use plain language
Formality	Be personal	Be impersonal
Thinking	Be logical	Show your thought process
Tone	Be serious	Be playful or humorous

Focus, concreteness, formality, tone—all of these difficult choices are yours to make. However, remembering your audience and purpose should make the decisions easier for you. You can also use Checklist 3.7 as you evaluate the first draft of your work. We have included many things that you can do; choose the ones that work for you.

CHECKLIST 3.7—EVALUATING YOUR FIRST DRAFT

Writer and Audience

- Are the tone and level of your writing appropriate for your audience? Read aloud some of the writing—how do you come across?

- Is the information load (amount of detail and explanation) right for your audience and purpose? How about the level of vocabulary? Have you met the information needs of the audience?

Purpose, Topic, and Pattern

- What was the level of purpose of this writing? What were the specific purposes? Did the pattern you chose allow you to accomplish your purposes?

- Has your writing given shape to the topic and defined its scope?

- Read your introduction and conclusion. What is the first impression your writing creates on the reader? What is the last impression? Do they fit together? Are these the effects you want?

- Pay special attention to the connections between pattern parts. Are transitions clear and smooth? Is the organization of the writing made clear to the reader?

Everything Else

- *Check every paragraph:* Should any long ones be divided? Should any short ones be combined?

- *Check every sentence:* Are all sentences punctuated correctly? Are any sentences too long to be clear? Have you varied the sentence structure to keep things interesting? Do you have errors in grammar or usage?

- *Check every word:* Is spelling correct? Capitalization? Do any words or phrases go "clunk?"

COMPUTERS AT WORK:

Planning and Drafting

Many word processing programs have an outlining feature that can help you in your planning and moving of the various pieces of your writing.

Another approach to planning and drafting is to use a hypertext program. This is a program that gives you the flexibility of a large number of index cards or spaces in which to write the various parts of your text. You can arrange and link these spaces in a variety of different ways, moving them around like physical index cards, and then drawing links between them. Some people find this a wonderful way to organize their writing. In that way, they can work on several different parts at the same time and then move them around and shape them into a final organization.

Whatever you do, be sure to save each document you have created, and when you cut something out save it in another file. You never can tell when you might need it.

Chapter Summary

There are different levels of purpose. Writings at Level One are designed to give information. Level Two writings go beyond giving facts to give interpretations, also. Level Three writings give advice or make recommendations. Preview questions for different patterns of organization let you consider the requirements of your writing as you are planning it. The writing checklist helps you to judge the value and completeness of your plan. It also reminds you that almost everything is your decision—a set of choices. Using a computer helps you to see several or many alternatives to each choice, without the time-consuming process of handwriting each possible choice.

In the next chapter you'll have a chance to expand your range by using everything you know how to do as a writer in writing and research projects in every course you take, as well as in your professional or career writing.

4 Writing for the Rest of Your Life

Do You Know:

- How to decide degree of detail and type of evidence required?
- How to make a research plan, from planning to finished product?
- How to use the same plan for writing assignments in various courses and situations?
- How to use a word processor as a file cabinet for your research?

Looking Ahead

Y ou've seen how to get started, how to keep going by giving shape to your writing, and how to plan the internal logic of your work—all useful things. When you learn something useful, you should use it every time you can. This chapter shows you how to do just that, with writings from math, science, social sciences, technology, and many other course areas.

You'll see how to approach writing and research projects to complete the job you're hired to do. We've included a one-page term paper assignment, along with examples of students' work and their teachers' comments. These are to show you that you can do almost any assignment in a variety of forms and still get the job done.

Doing Research Papers: From Planning to Evaluation

Establishing an organizational pattern may be the start—but is probably not the finish—of working with an assignment to produce the results you want. A pattern may establish a specific shape and organization, but it doesn't set degree of detail in the content you're looking for. Before you start work on an assignment, make sure you understand your instructor's expectations about the length and degree of detail involved. Find out what a complete answer will look like. Will it be a paragraph? Three to four paragraphs? Four to five pages? Forty-five pages? Determining length and degree of elaboration helps to answer the question "Is this what you want?"—before you are asked to do the work.

All instructors have read papers that are mere copies of encyclopedia articles or other sources. Students are astounded to discover that Xerography is not what was wanted or required. They are so caught up in searching for the information that they lose sight of what they must do with it—select it, give it shape, organize it, and present it in a different form or pattern for a particular audience for a specific purpose.

If you approach a research task with an audience, a purpose, and a pattern in mind, you are not as likely to get buried in data. In fact, if your plan or outline for the first draft is a pattern outline, you already have the system of organization ready for assembling the information found in research. If you can think of the pattern outline as a filing cabinet with drawers marked as pattern parts, you will see that when sources are found and notes are taken, there is already a place for them to be used.

Types of Evidence

In completing your assignment, you will also need to consider the types of evidence, support, or proof that will be required to complete the work. Many books distinguish between fact and opinion, but these two categories really oversimplify a complex issue. There are many kinds of evidence. The word "prove," for example, means different things in different contexts. Nor can the accuracy and validity of each type of evidence be taken for granted simply because a thing has been said or printed by someone. "Right" and "true" sometimes need qualifying as "right" according to whom, and "true" from what point of view.

Courtroom dramas, functional and real, often show two or more experts giving contradictory testimony, in the form of expert opinions, about the same case or circumstance. Following are some types of evidence and examples for each.

- **Observation or first-hand experience**—what we know (or think we know) through our own perceptions or experience

  San Francisco was cold—about 68 degrees—even in July.

- **Reported experience**—the observations of others reported to us

  My sister said San Diego was much warmer than San Francisco.

- **Cultural understandings or agreements**—agreed-upon or traditional ways of doing or considering things

  The continental U.S. is divided into four time zones.

- **Conclusions**—inferences made about the unknown, based on the known

  In New York, we always get the same weather Chicago had two days before.

- **Opinions**—expressions of attitude or judgment that show approval or disapproval (good or bad, right or wrong)

  It's disgusting the way those people wear their hair.

Whatever kinds of evidence you use, you will probably have to give credit to the source of that evidence.

Sources and Documentation Requirements

Many assignments students complete are from the textbook. We would call these single-source, secondary-source assignments. Usually, no documentation is required. Sometimes, copying directly from the text is allowed.

When you are asked to go beyond this single source, you will need to find out the number and types of sources you require. You will certainly need to know what documentation will be required, and what your rules are in this assignment for copying or paraphrasing from sources. You will also need to explain why these sources—number and type—contribute to your work. Are older and more recent views being compared? Are we looking for a balanced view from two or more perspectives? Do we want an interpretation of the original document? Do we want an expert opinion?

As a researcher and writer, you need to understand what constitutes **fair use.** You need to know what should be quoted, what can be paraphrased but still requires citation, and what can be used without citation.

If your teacher has not given you a documentation manual or model to work from, your library at school is sure to have one. A model commonly used is the Modern Language Association (MLA) model. In brief, documentation is streamlined in this way:

- A single "Works Cited" list appears at the end of the document, arranged in alphabetical order by author's last name.

- All references within the text are shown by giving the author's last name and the page(s) referred to in parentheses at the end of the sentence containing the cited material. This form of internal citation eliminates footnotes completely and replaces the bibliography with the Works Cited list.*

Developing a Research Plan

Almost any project, performance, or activity can be research based: contest entries, written or art compositions, interviews and consultations, oral history projects, dramatic and musical performances, such publications as booklets and brochures, training programs, and competitions.

Twenty years ago, unschooled researchers, working like medieval monks, copied by hand encyclopedia articles and thought they had a research paper. Ten years ago, equally unschooled researchers used more advanced technology to photocopy scores of pages of material they had no idea what to do with. Today, the CD ROM technology which allows students to *print* an entire volume of an encyclopedia has still not improved anyone's ability to select and shape the information. To conduct and report research effectively, you need to develop a research plan.

Inexperienced students seem to think of a research assignment as a one-stop shopping trip: Go to the library, get some stuff, bring it back. Done. Like the U.S. Postal Service, they just deliver what's already in the box. The stuff's there, or it isn't. The hard part of the process is locating the stuff—but don't worry, the librarians know where everything is.

Think of research as custom-building or constructing: The builder goes to the lumber yard, but doesn't buy a house and bring it back. Before the trip, the builder has a client and a blueprint or other design for the product. The builder shops to select what is needed to complete the designed construction. There may be changes along the way, but they are integrated into the plan that began the project. And the builder can't just dump all the materials on the lawn with a note that says "Some assembly required."

*See Example 4.8 later in this chapter for examples of works cited and internal citation.

Checkpoints. When doing research, you will want to establish many checkpoints along the way, so that you will be assured, step by step, that at the end, the whole thing isn't going to fall apart like a house of cards. The research guide that follows can help you see the entire process from designing to documenting your work. It can also serve as a master list for checkpoints along the way.

Like the writing process, the research process has stages of development that lead from the assignment or general topic to the finished product (see Table 4.1).

TABLE 4.1 THE PROCESS OF RESEARCH

- **Preparing:** Defining contexts, format, and guiding questions
- **Planning:** Previewing library and forming outline
- **Finding:** Selecting and gathering information
- **Drafting:** Writing the first version
- **Revising:** Evaluating midstream and making required changes
- **Evaluation:** Assessing content, organization, and everything else

Note: Before you go off to the library to work on an extensive paper or project, it is in your interest to submit a paper proposal for your instructor to review. A proposal would include all of the information, albeit in tentative form, included in the first stage of the process. In a page or two of informal writing, you would show your instructor the following:

CHECKLIST 4.1—PROJECT PROPOSAL

Preparing: Determining the size, shape, and purpose of the product
- Contexts: For what audience and purpose? What perspective?
- Present Knowledge: What do I already know about this topic?
- Tentative Format: Length? Pattern? Presentation? Documentation?
- Presearch Questions: What kinds of things do I need to find out?

Planning: Setting up the work
- Library Preview: What sources are available locally? By loan?
- Topic Overview: What is a general view on this topic or issue?

- Form Outline: Make an open outline in organizing pattern
- Method: Electronic and/or traditional research?
- Finding: Getting the necessary information
- Locating Sources: Retrieval for books, periodicals, other sources?
- Selecting: Definitely/possibly not useful for my purposes?
- Taking Notes: Quote or paraphrase? Documentation needs?

Drafting: Producing the first version of the final document
- Draft in Pattern: Complete text with quotes, citations, sources
- Evaluation Criteria:[†] Standards by which work will be done
- Documentation Check: Enough citations? Proper form? List complete?

Revising: Planning to modify for completeness, clarity, and correctness
- Content Changes: Enough information/sources? Right kinds?
- Organizational Changes: See "Preview Questions" again
- "Everything Else" Changes: Punctuation, wording, spelling, editing?

Final (or next) draft: Carrying out the revising plan for final draft
- Evaluation: Assessing the effectiveness of the product
- Content: Same as under "revising"—did the changes work?
- Organization: Same as under "revising"—did the changes work?
- Everything Else: Same as under "revising"—did the changes work?
- Documentation Requirements: Check MLA model style sheet.

Retrieval Systems. Depending on the technology available, retrieval systems vary for books, periodicals, and other media. In most libraries, the card catalog, *Reader's Guide to Periodical Literature,* and encyclopedia have been joined (if not replaced) by electronic retrieval systems. Some of these systems, because of their internal cross-referencing capabilities, can make a search much easier—if you know how to use the strategies available. For electronic data searches, you need to know how to use AND, OR, NOT, and other commands to control the scope of a search effectively. You will probably need guided practice in using the specific software available to you.

[†]See Chapter 7 on editing strategies.

Producing a Research Paper: A Case Study

The examples that follow show how one student researcher followed a plan to produce his research paper. As you follow his path, you can see how the work took shape as he went from planning to carrying out the plan for the final draft. First, a word on the assignment. The social studies instructor did *not* want a "typical" term paper.

Why not? Because typical term papers tend to be like the bad ones described earlier in this chapter: boring rehashes of encyclopedia entries without much real thinking on the part of the writer. In fact, in one research assignment we know about, a student handed in as a first draft a printout, word for word, of the Grolier Encyclopedia entry on his topic. He wasn't trying to be funny. He though that was research. He thought he was the U.S. postal service.

As veteran readers of research papers and projects, we'd say that papers poorly done are more often inadequately *written* than inadequately researched.

Hearing the words "term paper" does not make us anticipate curling up in front of the fire for a good read. (Picturing the *papers* curling up in the fire, unread, is more like it.)

The assignment that follows was our attempt to subordinate the research to everything else: the planning and thinking, and selecting and thinking, and writing and thinking involved. We wanted to break the "term paper" mold, so we limited the length and allowed—asked for—a variety of forms or schemes of internal logic. We also wanted to use the products of each student's work, so we required that the papers be presented in class. Following is the assignment as the students received it.

One-Page Research Paper Assignment

Directions: Your assignment is to compose a one-page paper based on your research into a topic you select. The second page of your paper will be a "Work Cited" list. Use the MLA model for internal citation in the paper: last name and pages, only. Write as many drafts as you need; make each as long as you like—until the final draft, which cannot exceed one typewritten page, about 250 words. Follow the specific instructions below. Plan, select, organize, present.

*Purpose: To present your research in an interesting, memorable way (so **do** something with the information).*

Audience: Classmates and fellow researchers and writers.

Role as Writer: You decide, but specify what it is.

General Topic: (Student's choice)

Specific Topic: You develop one from the general one.

Form: News, Topic-Aspect, Statement-Support, Question-Answer, How-To, Thesis-Proof, Opinion-Reason, Problem-Solution, Narrative, Dramatic

Types of Sources: Dictionaries, encyclopedias, atlases, almanacs, books of quotations, textbooks, other books, periodicals or media, people

Number of Sources: At least four: Two books, one quote, one other

Procedure: Freewrite, speculate, plan, develop pattern outline, read and take notes, compose, revise, edit, prepare documentation, print final copy

Additional Directions: Hand in draft with works cited list by (date). Hand in final draft by (date).

Students were given examples of quotations they might use for ideas, topics, viewpoints, and possible sources. A few thousand years ago, Cicero said this about war and conflicts: "An army is of little value in the field unless there are wise counsels at home."

Now here is the path that Jeff, our writer/researcher, took as he completed this assignment.

Preparing: Determining Size, Shape, and Purpose

Jeff began with a freewrite (an opening move) about "leadership," which led him to his general topic, Thomas Jefferson. From there, he sketched his plan (Examples 4.1 and 4.2).

EXAMPLE 4.1 FREEWRITE ABOUT RESEARCH PLAN

Preparing is the first step. Make sure there is adequate information on T. J. Then read the info. and don't copy the books, but form my own notes, factual to what was being said. Then, organize my notes.

EXAMPLE 4.2 OUTLINE OF RESEARCH PLAN

Research

1. Preparing
  a. Timed writing in class
  b. Review of sources (to be sure that an adequate number of sources were available)

2. Research
  (Since I recently visited Thomas Jefferson's estate, this part of the project involved reviewing my sources to refresh my memory on Monticello)
  a. Read information
  b. Outline (opinion-reason sheet)

3. First draft

4. Revision and "fine tuning"

5. Final Draft

Planning: Setting Up the Work from Planning Knowledge

A brief survey of the library and the pamphlets he had brought back from his trip to Monticello brought him to preliminary notes and more freewriting (Examples 4.3 and 4.4).

EXAMPLE 4.3 PRELIMINARY NOTES

(Outline)
Reflect his leadership qualities upon his home life

quote: "No occupation is as delightful to me as the culture of the
earth, and no culture comparable to that of the garden.
But though an old man I am but a young gardener."

House of two revisions
—interior
—all weather passageway
—Mulberry Row

Pamphlets
   1. Mullberry Row
   2. Thomas Jefferson's Monticello
   3. The Worlds of Thomas Jefferson at Monticello

Encyclopedia
   1. Groliers Encyclopedia

Individuals
   1. Tour guide at Monticello

EXAMPLE 4.4 MORE FREEWRITING

*Thomas Jefferson was the third President of the United States
as well as our second vice-president under John Adams. After
his presidency, he retired to his home in Monticello, Virginia in
Albermasle county. His home took 20 years to build and was a
work of art. Every corner was specifically built to his likings.
Because his favorite shape was the octagon, many of the rooms
in his house were in the shape of an octagon.*

Many people thought of him as a great <u>inventor</u>. He actually invented only one thing, that being the light-weight plow. He modified many European inventions.

Thomas Jefferson was not an inventor, although many people think of him as an inventor. He was, however, a very intelligent man!

I might use the opinion-reason format to write about Thomas Jefferson. I have a distinct opinion about his morals & mindset and can back these opinions up with reasons from my recent visit to his home in Monticello.

Drafting: Producing the First Version of the Final Document

Then Jeff drafted an outline in the pattern or internal logic he wanted to use, Opinion-Reason. This outline became the first draft (Example 4.5).

EXAMPLE 4.5 FIRST DRAFT

Writer: <u>Jeffrey Cohn</u>   *Purpose: <u>Informational</u>*
Audience: <u>Mr. Sotola</u>   *Register: <u>Semi-formal</u>*
Topic: <u>Thomas Jefferson</u>   *Pattern: <u>Opinion-Reason</u>*

Pattern Part

Monticello

<u>Opinion</u>   *Thomas Jefferson was an extremely intelligent individual in his political works. <u>His intelligence was reflected in his home life.</u>*

<u>Reasons</u>—Specific examples
Pattern part from Monticello

Reason   He was the architect of his own house. He designed every corner of the house, including much of his furniture.

Pattern Part

Reason   Using ideas from European architecture, he constructed a dome over the central hall, the first dome ever constructed in the United States.

Pattern Part

Reason   The all weather passageway which he constructed under the house was a unique style of architecture. It contained such things as the stables, the ice house, kitchen, servants room, etc. His idea behind this was to preserve the beautiful view.

Pattern Part

Reason   Thomas Jefferson's garden was proof of his intelligent planning and pride which he took in his estate. He grew a wide array of fruits and vegetables for his family and friends (pamphlet).

Revising: Modifying for Completeness, Clarity, and Correctness

Compare the first and final drafts to see what revisions Jeff made.

Final (or next) Draft: Carrying Out the Plan

Remember that the primary evaluation criterion was that the information be presented in an interesting way—interesting to the two instructors who would read them. Jeff's paper uses a traditional internal logic, but still shows his original thinking and writing. Opinions are based on research and personal experience.

EXAMPLE 4.6 FINAL DRAFT

<u>Thomas Jefferson at Monticello</u>

In Thomas Jefferson's political life, he proved to be one of the most intelligent men of all time. As Governor of Virginia, Secretary of State, our first Vice President, and our third president, his leadership qualities and intelligent thinking was respected by leaders around the world. His perseverance was reflected in his political life and his home life.

Thomas Jefferson's home at Monticello in Albermarle County, VA., was designed by Thomas Jefferson himself. The original house was begun in 1770 and took twelve years to complete. After visiting France, however, and observing some of the French architecture at the time, he returned to Monticello in 1793 with plans to revise his home. He doubled the size of the building by raising the ceilings and erecting a dome over the central hall. The revisions were completed sixteen years later in 1809 with an extremely detailed interior, all of which Jefferson designed himself. (<u>Groliers Ency-</u>

<u>clopedia</u>)

Jefferson was extremely interested in conserving space in

his home. One proof of this was the style of his beds. Each bed

was built into the wall. One foreign ambassador said, "I am

asked to come and speak at his home and forced to sleep in his

cupboards!" Other such things as a dumbwaiter, a seven-day

clock (built into the wall), and an all weather passageway

helped to conserve space around the house.

The all weather passageway was constructed under the

house and contained the stables, an ice house, the kitchen, the

servants' rooms, etc. It was placed there in order to conserve

space and to preserve the view. (<u>The Worlds of Thomas</u>

<u>Jefferson at Monticello</u>)

Thomas Jefferson took great pride in his gardening which

is found along Mullberry Row. It was here where his slaves

dwelled and his number of fruits and vegetables were grown.

(<u>Mullberry Row</u>) He once said, "No occupation is so delightful to me as the culture of the earth, and no culture comparable to

that of the garden. But though an old man I am but young a

gardener." (The Worlds of Thomas Jefferson at Monticello)

<u>Works Cited</u>

The Worlds of Thomas Jefferson at Monticello.
  Charlottesville, VA.: The Thomas Jefferson Memorial
  Foundation, 1993
Thomas Jefferson's Monticello.
  Charlottesville, VA.: The Thomas Jefferson Memorial
  Foundation, 1993
Mullberry Row.
  Charlottesville, VA.: The Thomas Jefferson Memorial
  Foundation, 1993
Groliers Encyclopedia. Computerized
  New York, NY: Grolier Electronic Publishing, Inc., 1992

Other Research-Based Papers

Now we'll give you more examples, finished products only, of creative papers that are research-based. All of them are responses to the one-page paper assignment. The first is a research poem, the next is a research dialogue, the third is a research interior monologue, and the fourth is a research reflection (Examples 4.7–4.10).

EXAMPLE 4.7 RESEARCH POEM

"All Great Alterations in Human
Affairs Are Produced by Compromise"
(Smith, pg. 294)

The Concordat of Worms ended
the Investiture Controversy. (<u>Americana</u>, pg. 340)
Henry Five and the bishops blended,
which the victor is still a mystery.

Both the Christians and the German state
had to give some of what they craved:
Henry- lay investiture's new fate,
the church- direct elections shaved. (Mills, pg. 117)

Results of the pledge were several:
imperial power abated,
piety of age came general,
and the medieval
empire slanted.
(Hollister, pgs. 183–187)

A change in 1122
would have affected both me and you.

Works Cited

1. Encyclopedia Americana. 1984 ed., Vol. 15, pg. 340.
2. Hollister, Warren C. Medieval Europe. New York: John
   Wiley & Sons, Inc., 1978, pg. 183–187.
3. Mills, Dorothy. The Middle Ages. New York: G. P. Putnam's
   Sons, 1935, pg. 117.
4. Smith, Sydney. The Home Book of Quotes. New York: Dodd,
   Mead, & Co., 1949, pg. 204.

EXAMPLE 4.8 RESEARCH DIALOGUE

A Tour of France

Anne Everett

We will now tune in to an interesting conversation between an American priest, Father Smith and his tour guide,
Pierre. They are on the R.E.R., the "super-metro" of France,
on which you can see the entire country in a matter of hours
(Kane-Brauns, January 10, 1994).

Pierre: France is known for its unusual geometric shape.

Father Smith: Many French writers refer to it as a
"l'hexagon," because of the neat, six-sided outline of the
country (Balerdi, Susan p. 7).

Pierre: Yes, Father Smith, that is correct. (Turning to
other passengers) We have just left the Central Basin, the
long, flat province of France connecting Paris to the middle of
the country. We are now entering the province of Normandy.
These gently, rolling hills. . . .

Father Smith: (interrupting) . . . they yield some of the finest apples in France, to make their wine and cider. It is also noted for its abundance of dairy products (Balerdi, Susan p. 9).

Pierre: You are exactly right. And . . .

Father Smith: As it says in Luke 3:3, "Every valley must be filled up, every hill and mountain leveled off." (Good News Bible Luke 3:3)

Pierre: Yes, Father. I see but I would appreciate if you would let me . . .

Father Smith: Oh, yes. Excuse me.

Pierre: (starting to get annoyed) Thank you. Now as we continue traveling south, we enter Les Landes. You may notice that these beautiful beaches have great pine trees lining the coast. In the eighteenth century, the farmers in Les Landes were afraid that erosion from the ocean would wash away their farms. So they planted a pine forest all along the coast (Encyclopedia Britannica p. 265).

Father Smith: (to Pierre) You know, you look a little pale. Why don't you take my seat. I'll finish this tour.

Pierre: Well, no. That's okay.

(Father Smith gently pushes Pierre into his seat and takes the microphone.)

Father Smith: Now we are entering the final leg of our journey, my favorite province in France, le Midi-Pyrenees. It is where the Alps meet the Pyrenees. You are also able to see many small villages perched on top of these rocky mountains. Some of these houses are over 2000 years old! This concludes our trip for today. Thank you for coming and have a nice day! (Balerdi, Susan p. 10).

Pierre: (standing up as the bus is clearing) Very nice job, Father Smith. You really do know a lot about France's geography. Just don't expect my paycheck, "Monsieur Tour Guide!"

Works Cited

Balerdi, Susan. France: The Crossroads of Europe. Dillon Press, Inc. 1984 p. 7–20.

Encyclopedia Britannica. Vol. IV. p. 265–266—France. Encyclopedia Britannica, Inc., Chicago—1977.

<u>Good News Bible</u>. American Bible Society, New York, 1976
     Gospel according to Luke, Chapter 3, verse 3.

Kane–Brauns, Mrs. Suzanne.—interview (1/10/94).

EXAMPLE 4.9 RESEARCH INTERIOR MONOLOGUE

Life in America—Life in Another World
by Umm Saad
as told to Megan Kavanaugh

When, in 1993, my brother, Ahmad bin Abdullah, invited

me to visit him in the United States for my thirty-second

birthday, I eagerly accepted. I was fluent in English and would

be staying with Ahmad, so I foresaw no problems.

As soon as I stepped off the plane, however, I realized

that I had been wrong. In my homeland of Saudi Arabia, it is

impolite for a stranger to talk to a woman, yet in the Ameri-

can airport, men kept attempting conversation with me. Then I

received my biggest shock—my taxi driver was a woman.

Saudi women don't drive; in fact, if a policeman ever caught a woman driving, her husband would be arrested for allowing her to drive (McCarthy, 30, 74).

I was greeted at my brother's door by my 17-year-old niece. That she was single and still living at home confused me. I was married at age 15, an average age for a Saudi woman. My husband honored me and my family by offering a dowry of four camels and nine sheep (McCarthy, 75–76).

During my stay in America, I realized all of the opportunities that Saudi women miss. I went to a restaurant where men and women sit together, saw schools where both sexes are taught in the same room, and met women who worked in fields that deal with men. During my one week stay in America I met more men than I had met in my entire life, for Saudi women rarely see men outside their immediate family (Epstein, 321).

My stay in the U.S. showed me that although Saudi men feel that the "woman is the lesser man," (Tennyson, "The Lord of Burleigh") Americans have "faith in womankind"

(Tennyson, "The Revenge"). I will miss this trust when I

return to Saudi Arabia.

WORKS CITED

Epstein, Cynthia. "Woman" The World Book Encyclopedia,
　　(Chicago: World Book, Inc., 1985) Vol. 21.
McCarthy, Kevin. Saudia Arabia: A Desert Kingdom (Minne-
　　apolis: Dillon Press, Inc., 1986.)
"Tennyson, Alfred Lord: 'The Lord of Burleigh'" The Oxford
　　Dictionary of Quotations, (New York: Oxford University
　　Press, 1980) p. 539.
"Tennyson, Alfred Lord: 'The Revenge'" The Oxford Book of
　　Quotations, (New York: Oxford University Press, 1980)
　　p. 532.

EXAMPLE 4.10 RESEARCH REFLECTION

Isn't this just wonderful! I should have expected this from
the start. If only they hadn't evolved into such intelligent
creatures! Well, at least they all seem to think that they're so
incredibly intelligent, but . . . oh, never mind. Anyway, it's
happening already. And I only had them fooled for sixty
thousand years. Not very long at all on a universal time scale.
I always thought, or hoped, really, that it would take longer
than that for them to figure this entire situation out.

You see, they didn't used to be this way. They really
weren't all that bright in the beginning. They did evolve from
primates, you know. It was quite simple, really. For example,
death. Not a very difficult concept to grasp. One day you're

quite active, next day you're stone dead. So, naturally, they began to wonder about this mysterious phenomenon, inquisitive creatures that they are. And, since their limited anatomical knowledge left them with absolutely no hope of determining the cause of this unfortunate circumstance, they made something up, supported by the theory stating "If God did not exist, it would be necessary to invent him." (Voltaire, <u>Epitre a Auteur du Livre des Trois Imposteurs</u>)

At first, it was nature. You know, the rocks, the trees, the water. Yes, water spirits, definitely water spirits. Animism is the theory one would logically imagine to explain natural phenomena, right? But, as they ever so slowly gained in intellectual power, they began to wonder not only about what made the wind blow, or where a newborn child comes from, but things like the origin of the universe, the existence of subatomic particles, multiple time oriented realities, simple stuff like that. So, of course, water spirits just didn't quite cover it any more. (<u>The World Book</u>, Volume 16)

This is where I come in. The Supreme Being, creator of everything. End of story. Well, not quite. You see, I was able to hold their inquisitiveness in check for a while with a few neat tricks like the Inquisition. After all, if you kill all of the intellectuals in a given world, who's going to tell the rest of them that I really can't logically exist. But, the intellectuals countered with the Renaissance, and look at the result! Philosophers and scientists of all kinds are allowed to think and voice their thoughts freely! Professors teach the theory of evolution to their students! There's no doubt about it. They're discovering the truth! (W. Durant, <u>The Age of Faith</u>)

Why is this happening? What's wrong with them? After all, I must lend them some sense of security. Anyone would feel better if he or she had their own supreme being watching over them, right? "Naught but God can satisfy the soul," right? (P. J. Baily, <u>Festus: Heaven</u>) Of course I'm right, I'm supreme! But they don't seem to think so anymore, or at least not all of them. But why? After all, everything I stand for is so right for everyone, so practical. Males labor to support the females, who need not pursue an education since their main purpose is to raise their children, which they conceived as a result of procreational, and definitely not recreational, 'knowing.' And there will be several of these children since the evils of contraception, and, worse yet, abortion, are strictly not permitted. (The Bible, Genesis)

Despite all of these wonderful morals I've provided for them, and the emotional support, and all of the 'knowingly' frustrated men in black, they're losing faith. And you do, of course, know what the consequences of that are, don't you. Well, "Religion without mystery ceases to be religion," as one of them so accurately stated it. (W. T. Manning, Sermon Feb. 2, 1930) And that is definitely not good for my mental health. You see, when they no longer believe in me, I simply cease to exist.

—Joshua Tallent

Bibliography

Books

1. The Bible, King James Version. The American Bible Society, New York, New York, 1952.
2. Kelly, Werner. The Bible as History. William Morrow and Company, New York, New York, 1956.
3. Durant, William. The Age of Faith. Simon and Schuster, New York, New York, 1950.

Quotes

1. "Religion without mystery ceases to be religion." Bishop William Thomas Manning, Sermon (February 2, 1930).

2. "Naught but God can satisfy the soul." P. J. Baily, <u>Festus: Heaven</u>.

3. "If God did not exist, it would be necessary to invent him." Voltaire, <u>Epitre a Auteur du Livre des Trois Imposteurs</u>, November 10, 1770.

All Quotes Taken From Stevenson, Burton. <u>The Home Book of Quotations</u>, Dodd, Mead, and Company. New York, New York, 1949.

Other

1. <u>The World Book Encyclopedia</u>, Volume 16, Pages 216–226, World Book, Chicago, Illinois, 1990.

Writing Across the Curriculum

If you can do something interesting in one page, imagine what you can accomplish in five or ten. And you can—and will probably have to—write papers of various kinds in most academic areas over the course of your education. The rest of this chapter offers you a selection of topics and activities taken from different disciplines in the curriculum. We think you will find that your writing, planning, and organizing abilities won't just "come in handy" in these courses other than English; they'll be the key to your success in them.

Some of the following assignments are specific; others are quite general. Some require a particular form or approach; others leave almost all decisions up to you. If you want to (or have to) write in science, mathematics, social sciences, and other courses you are now taking or will take later on, these activities can get you started. Even if you do not have writing requirements in other courses at this time, you might still want to show your range in your portfolio by including a work or works from other fields.

Thus far we've focused on two kinds of portfolios, your working portfolio and the final or presentation one. There is a third, and it is more important than the others. The third portfolio is *you*—the repertoire of writing abilities and techniques you can call on. Your final portfolio may be presented a few times, but you, the living version of the working portfolio, will present yourself in speaking and writing a million more times. You are the one portfolio that will never be "finished."

As you look through the activities that follow, plan to complete the ones that will add something significant to your repertoire. Think "range." Think "depth."

Working Together

One thing you might want to add to your repertoire is a collaborative work. For any of the Assignments for Subject Areas, you might work with classmates to produce a collaborative work or an array of works in response to one assignment.

Begin by choosing one to three people to work with. Select an assignment that suits all of you, and then decide whether to produce: (a) a single piece of writing worked on by the group, or (b) an array of responses to a single assignment.

Taking control as a writer means making decisions. If you decide to try something as a group, you'll have a chance to make dozens of decisions about what to produce, how to get started, how to keep going, and how to know when you're finished.

A side effect of working on a group effort is that you will make some discoveries about your own ways of working, both as a group member and as an individual.

Assignments for Subject Areas

Art and Music: Writing for Learning

Write a note to your instructor explaining how you practiced a difficult passage or piece (or how you went about composing a challenging piece of artwork or music). Be sure to give specific information about (a) the different strategies you tried; (b) what you learned from trial and error; and (c) how successful you were. Write at least two paragraphs of complete sentences, perhaps eight to ten sentences in all. The title of your note could be, "How I Tried to _____ ."

Art and Music: Organizing for Presentation

Write a proposal for your grade on a specific project or performance. Consider:

• The time you spent

- The effort it took
- The interest you showed
- The responsibility you took
- The difficulty of the part or project
- The quality of the final product
- Any other factors you think should help determine your grade

When you write about your work, make specific comments about the project or performance, and give evidence—examples from your work—to support your opinion. Remember that you're making a case for your grade, and you'll have to prove it to your reader. Write as yourself. Your audience is your instructor, the person who has the responsibility and the authority to grade your project or performance.

To help you plan your evidence, make an outline using an Opinion-Reason pattern (following). As you think about your work, jot down the ideas you want to use in the places where they will best fit. Use your own notebook paper. When you have enough ideas and evidence in the outline, go ahead and write your proposal on another page, following the organization you used in the outline.

OPINION-REASON PATTERN

Opinion (your overall evaluation of the project or performance):
_____

Reason #1 (first factor and evidence): _____

Reason #2 (next factor and evidence): _____

Reason #3 (another factor and evidence): _____

Recommendation (summary and grade you should receive): _____

Business, Home Economics, Technology: Writing for Learning

A machine you need to use is not working properly. What would you do to try to get it to work?

Choose one machine or piece of equipment you normally use in this class, and give it a problem: pick a way for the machine to fail to work. (For example, if you normally used a microscope in a science class, you might one day discover that it wouldn't focus.) On your own notebook paper, write down your perception of the problem in a sentence or two.

After you identify what doesn't work, tell what you would try to do to get it to work. Quickly list the steps you'd take to try to correct the problem with the machine. The title of your list could be, "How I'll Try to Fix the _____ ."

Business, Home Economics, Technology: Organizing for Presentation

Even though they receive separate paychecks, very few workers really work alone. Almost all jobs are linked to other jobs, making workers dependent on each other whether or not they want to be. That applies to architects, brokers, caterers . . . down to zookeepers.

What are the effects of interdependence? Interdependence means you have to rely on others; your performance affects others; others' performance affects you; and cooperation, compromise, and negotiation are part of the job. Since the performance of the group is affected by each person in it, a person who is not effective at working in the group hurts everybody, like a clumsy or uncooperative player on a team.

What about you? What kind of team player are you? What kinds of problems do you have in trying to work with other people? What could you do to improve your ability to work within the group you are in now—this class?

On your own paper, develop a Problem-Solution outline similar to the one following by completing the sentences and adding details for each part. Be sure to give specific examples, cases, situations, or illustrations for each part of the outline. When the outline is completed with all the information you need, use it as the basis for your finished writing: a one- to two-page paper of advice to yourself. A secondary audience is your instructor, who will also read it.

PROBLEM-SOLUTION PATTERN

Problem: My biggest problem in working with other people is _____ .

Effects: The results or effects of this problem are _____ .

Causes: I think this problem is caused by _____ .

Solution: A way to solve this problem would be to _____ .

Significance: The benefits, both for me and the group, of solving this problem would be _____ .

Health and Physical Education: Writing for Learning

What sports or games do you play best? Soccer? Tennis? Checkers? Monopoly? Choose two or three sports, games, or activities that you play well. What makes you skillful or effective at them? Try to identify a specific ability that makes you competent. Write a paragraph or two to identify the ability and show how it makes you good.

Health and Physical Education: Organizing for Presentation

"It looks easy." People who watch a game or sports activity cannot always appreciate how difficult and complicated the activity may be. Think of a game or sport that you play that might look simple to a spectator, but is not so simple for the player.

Then, write an article for spectators of the sport or activity. Write from the point of view of an experienced player of the activity. In the article, explain some of the hidden difficulty or complexity players must deal with. The article will appear on the sports page.

Consider the most important subskills of the sport or activity. Think about the best players you know in the activity—what makes them great? Think about specific situations that are difficult or complex for the player.

Use a Topic-Aspect pattern to organize your ideas. The opening sentences given below are just to get you started. After you complete the outline, write your article for the sports page.

TOPIC-ASPECT PATTERN

Topic: The sport (or game) of _____ is not as simple as it looks. To be good at it, a person must have competence in a number of subskills.

Aspect 1: _____

Aspect 2: _____

Aspect 3: _____

Application: _____

Languages: Writing for Learning

In arithmetic, 1 + 1 usually adds up to 2. In language, that isn't always the case. The Spanish expression "No hay de que" includes these words:

no = no, not

hay = there is, there are

de = from, of

que = who, what

However, "No hay de que" does not mean, *No there is from what.* Instead, it means something like, *Don't mention it* or *No big deal.*

How can an expression mean something different from the sum of its words? Try to work out an answer to this question. Think of and write down a few expressions in English that "don't add up" and try to suggest how they can mean something different from what they seem to say.

Languages: Organizing for Presentation

A baby cries in the crib. A president delivers an inaugural address. Your parent gives a lecture. A girl sings at a concert. A boy carves a name in a tree. Someone at your table asks you to pass the salt. What do all of these events have in common? They all involve people communicating—using language to get what they want.

The seven language purposes listed below come from Michael Halliday, a language theorist. His theory is that these seven purposes explain why we use language. He says we use language:

1. To get things done
2. To get along with other people
3. To control the behavior of other people
4. To learn about ourselves
5. To learn about the world around us
6. To play, invent, or create an imaginary world
7. To produce knowledge about the world of reality[‡]

What do *you* want? How do you use language to try to get what you want? Explain to your classmates how you have used language in three of these ways during the past week. Give a specific example or situation for each one, and tell if each attempt was successful.

Use a Statement-Support outline (similar to the one shown below) to organize your ideas, and then write a one- or two-page paper to explain how you used language for at least three of these purposes during the past week.

STATEMENT-SUPPORT PATTERN

Statement: _____
Support 1: _____
Support 2: _____
Support 3: _____
Application: _____

[‡]Halliday, M. A. K. *Learning How to Mean.* New York: Elsevier North Holland, Inc., 1975.

Mathematics: Writing for Learning

If . . . I have to solve the following set of linear equations without using graph paper . . .

$$x + y = 7$$
$$x - y = 3$$

Then . . . I would (*explain how you might try to do it*)

Because . . . (*use your knowledge of mathematics to explain why this would work*)

Mathematics: Organizing for Presentation

Write the plans for a class presentation in which you will show how a problem can be solved in three different ways—using three different solution strategies.

For each solution, give all necessary steps and explain how you get from one step to the next, as well as why you are allowed to take that step. Remember that some of your audience will have had some experience with some of the methods, but that you will need to be able to explain everything you do.

Use a Thesis-Proof pattern to organize your presentation. The thesis will outline the problem requirements, and each proof will illustrate one solution method. In the Significance section, explain how and when (with what types of problems) each solution method can best be used.

Make handouts for students of all the parts they need to see to follow your presentation. Your presentation should take about 5 minutes, with another 3 minutes for questions from the audience.

THESIS–PROOF PATTERN

Thesis: ⸺⸺⸺
Proof 1: ⸺⸺⸺
Proof 2: ⸺⸺⸺
Proof 3: ⸺⸺⸺
Significance: ⸺⸺⸺

Science: Writing for Learning

Draw a vertical line down a sheet of notebook paper. In four minutes, list everything you think you know about *mitosis* in the column on the left. When time is up, quickly write anything you think you know about *meiosis*—make it up, if you need to—in the column on the right: What is it?

How does it work? What might happen? Don't worry about being accurate. Just try to fill the column with "facts" about meiosis.

Bill Mitosis and Winnie Meiosis have led different lives. Each of them has divided, but in different ways and with different results. On another sheet of notebook paper, write their differing stories. For each character, be sure to tell:

- at what point the copied chromosomes separate from the originals,

- how many cells are produced by the division, and

- how many chromosomes exist in the nucleus of each new cell.

Each story is already begun below. Finish each one by writing two or three paragraphs which include the details listed above.

The Story of Bill Mitosis	**The Story of Winnie Meiosis**
Bill felt that it was time for him to divide.	Winnie felt that it was time for her to divide.

Science: Organizing for Presentation

You have read about or seen a demonstration involving a change. How can you determine what caused the change? Do you have a hypothesis about the cause or causes of the change? Can you think of a way to test your hypothesis through an experiment?

Think of a laboratory report form, only in reverse of the usual way you would use it. Instead of recording your lab work, **plan** it with the lab report form model below. Be sure to think about the observations you would need to make and the conclusions you would need to draw to decide whether to confirm, reject, or modify your hypothesis.

Work out your ideas on your own paper, using the form below as a guide, and then describe the experiment you would conduct to test your hypothesis about the cause (or causes) of the change.

LABORATORY REPORT

The change you observed: _____

Your hypothesis about the cause(s): _____

The experiment you would design: _____

Materials: _____

Methods: _____

Conclusions you might expect to draw:

If _____ , my hypothesis is confirmed because _____ .

If _____ , my hypothesis is rejected because _____ .

If _____ , my hypothesis is modified to _____ because

_____ .

LABORATORY WRITEUP

Observation of change: _____

Hypothesis about cause(s): _____

Experiment to test the hypothesis: _____

Materials: _____

Methods: _____

Conclusions about hypothesis: _____

Social Studies: Writing for Learning

Start your research project by selecting a topic that interests you. Then you will explore that topic and give it some shape. Vertically divide a sheet of notebook paper into four columns: people, places, times, and events.

When you first find something interesting—a person, place, time, or event—in the list of topics or other sources given to you by your instructor, write it in the appropriate column. Then, start to fill in the other columns with information. As you go on, the information should get more and more specific, thus defining and narrowing the topic. As the chart fills, you are also generating a valuable list of cross-references that will help you in your research.

If you are allowed to use general resources (such as your textbook) during this stage, your chart will contain accurate information. If you must complete the chart on your own, treat the information—what you think you know about the topic—as hypothetical. Your later research will allow you to confirm, reject, or modify your hypothetical knowledge.

As you do early research and discover that Alexander the Great (person) didn't make it to the Crimean war (event), which wasn't held in France (place) during the time of the Children's Crusade (event and time), you will be able to replace these ideas with more accurate information.

Topic ——————————————————

People   Places   Times   Events

COMPUTERS AT WORK:

Setting Up a File Cabinet for Research

As you first block out the idea for a paper you should make a set of categories or "folders" for your project. These would include the following:

- Resources (including bibliography),
- Reading notes and quotations (labelled by source),
- Reflections and ideas, and
- Extras (pieces that might be useful).

Be sure to use a separate floppy for the project and be sure to back everything up.

You will need to create files for your project that include spaces for each of these. You can use your word-processing program for each of these or you can use a separate database program and an outline or hypertext program.

The database program will let you create a separate entry for each book or article or each interview that you have done. The program works like a stack of 3" × 5" cards in that you can create separate cards for each segment and then search through them and organize them any way you want to. Some of these programs are particularly useful for formulating your final bibliography in that they will set it up according to the bibliographic style that you need to use. You must be sure to include all the necessary information the first time, however, so you don't have to go back to the library and check things again.

Your library may have a number of electronic databases that you can search through in order to find sources on your topic. These can be useful to you in preparing your research, but you should check to make sure that the article or book you want is available.

After you have done the various pieces of research and advance writing, you are then able to arrange the segments into the final draft in the order that you want. You probably have the feature on your word processing program to import these segments or copy and paste them. Any pieces that you decide not to use you can save and then consider later when you come to the revision.

Tip: Make sure you label each section or file so that it will be easy to find.

Chapter Summary

At the start of an assignment, make clear for yourself the length, degree of detail, and type of evidence required, as well as the method of documentation your instructor wants you to use. Remember that any activity can be research based, even if it isn't called a "research" assignment.

The power of using a research plan—from planning to final draft—is that it will guide you through the entire process. In the assignments from other areas of study, you can see that the same general approach we use to "English" or "composition" writing assignments can be used for assignments across the curriculum, and beyond it for professional or work-related writing.

For research-based writings, you can use several features of your word-processing program and other programs to carry your work through to the finish.

The next chapter will go into detail on writing about literature.

5 Writing about Literature

Do You Know:

- The reasons for writing about literature?
- How to keep a response journal?
- How to turn your questions into a formal paper?
- How to write up various literature projects?

Looking Ahead

This chapter will discuss one of the main kinds of writing that goes on in English courses: writing about what you read, particularly writing about literature. It will focus on both the informal writing and the formal writing that you may be assigned.

We will examine the various kinds of questions that people ask about their reading and see how these questions can be turned into critical writing. We will also examine how you can prepare various other literature-related projects for your portfolio.

few years ago, one of our children asked this question: "If Ms. B. [the instructor] wants to know the answers to these questions [about a novel that had been assigned], Dad, why doesn't she read it herself?" It's probably a question that you have asked, too. If the point about literature is to read books, stories, poems, plays, and other pieces, what's all this writing about? Is it just a form of testing to see whether you have read it?

When most people answer the question, "What are you reading?" they are talking about the reading of a poem or a story in a magazine or a book; or perhaps about the reading of a novel. These are the sorts of things that people pick up voluntarily. They are surrounded by a cover, a dust-jacket with some information about the author, and perhaps a brief introduction or even a footnote or two. The reader picks up a text and chooses to read it. We call this reading for pleasure. Sometimes you are even encouraged to read for pleasure in school.

When you read a particular story for pleasure you are not often asked much about the reading. A friend may ask, "Did you like it?" Somebody else might ask, "What's it about?" But that is about all that happens, and your answers don't have to be very long.

When you look at the same story in a literature anthology, you will find that it has new surroundings. There is a unit or chapter introduction, along with a text introduction accompanied by biographical and other contextual information. Surrounding the text will be notes and vocabulary items. Following the text you may find vocabulary drills, comprehension questions, in-class activities, and several writing assignments. There may also be an illustration or two. Perhaps only 50% of the text material is produced by the original author—even less if it is a lyric poem. The rest is produced by unknown hordes like us.

Put very simply, the physical text in a literature classroom frequently becomes a different object from what it is in the outside world. Even the class sets of a paperback novel will have various school insignia grafted on to them to signal that the readers are part of a different culture. This difference suggests a difference between the reading of the text in a classroom and the reading of a text in a living room.

Literature as a Course of Study

In your courses you are expected to learn something, and other people determine whether you have done so by giving tests. So it is with the study of literature, but what are you supposed to learn? You are expected, certainly, to learn the names of books and writers and characters and literary terms. Sometimes you are supposed to remember facts about what you have read for tests and other final examinations. In addition, you will need to pick up the correct meaning of terms like *plot, setting, imagery,* and *symbol.*

Another major part of what you are supposed to learn covers the wide variety of ways by which you let people know what you think (and feel) about what you have read. This is often called your **response**—or your ability to say what the piece of literature means to you, how good it is, how it relates to your life, and how it is put together. You are not just reading in a closet but bringing an impression of what is read out into the open. Like any school subject, your literature course involves public acts in which you must be articulate about what you have read and also about the procedures and strategies that led you to your conclusions about what you have read. Proofs are not necessary in mathematical applications outside of class; essays about one's reading of a text are not required after reading every library book.

You are also expected to show that you have developed some habits as a reader. In literature classes, a "good" reader is supposed to want to continue reading a book that has been selected. A good reader is supposed to relate what she is reading to her life or to the world around her. A good reader is supposed to read a variety of types of books, and to read more difficult books. She can't just stay with mysteries or *Star Trek.* A good reader is supposed to be careful about making judgments about characters or situations. A good reader is expected to pay attention to the words and phrases in the book. A good reader is supposed to be able to predict and then test those predictions. A good reader is supposed to come up with an interpretation of the book or story. A good reader is supposed to treat a story differently from a textbook. Above all, a good reader is expected to volunteer to talk and write about the text; you can't respond as our child did in the beginning of this section—and you shouldn't simply copy *Cliff's Notes* as if it were the only interpretation.

So, when you prepare the part of your portfolio that shows what you are like as a student of literature, make sure that you show evidence of what you know, what sort of a reader and responder you are, and what habits you have developed. The main ways to show these aspects of yourself are through response journals or reading logs, through formal papers, and through other projects.

Response Journals

The idea behind response journals or reading logs is that you should keep a record of what book you are reading and what you think about it during each session that you sit down with it. You can't wait until you finish the book to start thinking about it—any more than you would wait until you were dead ("see how it ends") before you thought about your life.

Normally, the response journal begins with the name of the book and its author, and it may be done in a paragraph format (See Example 5.1) or a double-column format (see Example 5.2).

As in most journals, you need to indicate the date and time that you did the reading, and your comments, reactions, jottings of quotes that you liked or didn't like, and references to other books or films that you have read or watched.

EXAMPLE 5.1 RESPONSE JOURNAL ENTRY (PARAGRAPH FORMAT)

Jane Austen/Mansfield Park

Nov 7

I think that Fanny can be seen as a Cinderella character because she is taken into a family where she is somewhat pampered. Not to the extent at which she gets everything that she wants but that she no longer lives in poverty and her wish that her brother succeeds is granted. She, like Cinderella, has two wicked step-sisters. However, Fanny's "step-sisters" do not treat her as as much of an outcast as they did in the beginning of their relationship with her as children. She eventually gets her prince charming although Edmund doesn't seem to be as much of a charming man as the fairy-tale prince. Fanny also has a wicked stepmother in the form of the dreaded Mrs. Norris. This woman who is actually Fanny's aunt and her wicked cousins all meet their deserved ends. However I am not sure that Fanny's attainment of Edmund is really what she deserves.

Nov 11

We root for Fanny not because we agree with her decisions but because she is seen to be a good individual. She is a moral creature and tries not to be a bother to anyone. She is kind to everyone even to those who might not deserve her kindness nor do they return it. Jane Austen pulls this off because she makes Fanny into a character which is passive. She in a way is pushed to the back of our minds and we don't think of her in the same way that we think about characters such as Mrs. Norris, Julia and the rest. We don't really form an opinion of Fanny until we are asked to do so by an outside force.

Nov 12 [after the teacher's comment]
By outside force I mean either a question asked, like one in which the reader is supposed to give an interpretation of Fanny's character or thoughts on Fanny's character after one may have read a criticism on Mansfield Park. Also when other characters in the book give their opinion of Fanny, the reader must muse over that opinion and form an opinion of their own in order to see how they feel about the character which gave the primary opinion.

—K. K.

In a two-column format, the first column usually records the place in the book to which the entry is referring (by page number or short incident description) and the second column is used for responses.

EXAMPLE 5.2 RESPONSE JOURNAL ENTRY
(TWO-COLUMN FORMAT)

John Steinbeck/ The Pearl

Facts	*Feelings*
Kino, Juana, Coyotito-baby	*Might be a parable, a biblical story*

Facts	Feelings
Setting—near dark, almost morning, a village w/pigs and roosters.	
People of his made songs. Kino has his personal songs. Juana very good wife. She cares for her family goat outside brush house.	Feelings in heart and soul.
	Must be poor Indians living with their people in the village.
Kino considers his family, Juana, Coyotito, his life, his house, his songs.	Probably he's happy with what he's got and doesn't desire for anything else.

The Whole

Kino—young, strong, black hair. Kino and Juana have a great relationship. They don't need to use words to communicate. They must love each other a lot. Scorpion—near Coyotito's hanging box. Song of Evil.	Shows that he's able to do anything he desires as well as that he's immature in life experience.
	Kino is probably feeling, or sensing the danger of the scorpion.
Juana—chanting magic and praying	Their religions and beliefs.

Facts	*Feelings*
Kino tried to get the scorpion, but was unsuccessful. It fell and struck the baby.	
Kino took all his anger out on the scorpion. He pounded on it w/ his fist till it was mushed.	Must have taken all his anger out on it. He was sensing enemy, because the song of enemy was in his head.
Juana was comforting the baby. Kino fell in the way.	
Juan Thomas—Kino's brothers Neighbors gathered around	Must be either nosy or helping each other.
Decided to go to the doctor.	Juana is strong and she's the one that decides.

Remember that a response journal should not be simply a plot summary. Instructors are not interested in seeing that. Instead, they want to see what sorts of concerns and questions you might have about your reading. Your own reading of the book is at issue here. Instructors want to know *that* you are thinking; they also want to know *what* you are thinking and *why*. The student who wrote the journal in Example 5.2 was exploring character and motivation. This preliminary work gave her a good start on writing a character sketch of Kino and answering a test question on the relationships within Kino's family and between the family and the rest of the village and the outside world.

Example 5.3 shows a more elaborated version of the response journal taken from a course that focused on exploring critical interpretations. The students had been discussing the feminist quest model of interpretation and were comparing it with the interpretive framework of existential

EXAMPLE 5.3 READING LOG FOR "THE YELLOW WALLPAPER"

Text Reference (or *Issue*)	*Feminist Quest Model*
pg 180—"I get unreasonably angry with John sometimes. I'm sure I never used to be so sensitive. I think it is due to this nervous condition. "But John says if I feel so I shall neglect proper self-control; so I take pains to control myself—before him, at least, and that makes me very tired."	—She is being *repressed* by John and feels she is wrong if she doesn't please him (although she apparently doesn't realize this)—*nervous condition*—'sane' response to destructive society?—she acts differently around husband—fear?
pg 181—". . . When you follow the lame uncertain curves for a little distance they suddenly commit *suicide*—*plunge off* at outrageous angles, *destroy themselves* in unheard-of contradictions . . . I should hate it myself if I had to live in this room long."	—She may be seeing the pattern of her own *life* in the pattern of the *wallpaper*—the mention of "suicide" and "destroy themselves" may indicate the taking of her own (or someone else's) life as a result of her *repression*
pg 183—"I used to feel that if any of the other things looked too fierce, I could always hop into that chair and be safe."	—"Chair"—inanimate object seen as 'strong friend' w/which to escape male-dominated society (perhaps her *father* was like *John*)
pg 185—"And it is like a woman stooping down and creeping about behind that pattern. I don't like it a bit. I wonder—I began to think—I wish John would take me away from here!"	—The woman behind the pattern could be herself she's seeing—feeling *repressed* by something, not knowing that it's John doing this to her

Alienation Model	"My Comment"
—*Psychological Alienation*—her true self is lost underneath the "person she is for John" —She *compensates* her *psycho. alien.* by writing	—I think the *Feminist Quest* model fits better because she seems to be more "repressed" than she is "alienated"
—*Philosophical Alienation*— John's causing of *psycho. alien.* may be causing her to think there is "no where to turn" and that she should kill herself	—I think both models work well w/this text reference (maybe the *Alienation* model fits a little bit better) and both seem to point to suicide (or some other form of death) in the future
—Being alienated by John (male society) causes her to seek comfort in inanimate objects (i.e. *chair* and *wallpaper*)	—*Both* models work well with this TR —Both point to the fact that she is trying to escape her repressive/alienating relationships
—She doesn't realize that it's John that's alienating her (psychologically) —She still looks to him for support	—*Feminist Quest* works better— reference to the woman "helps" this model a lot

—Sean Gifford

alienation. The assignment was to compare the two interpretive approaches as they might apply to a story, in this case "The Yellow Wallpaper" by Charlotte Perkins Gilman. One student used the response journal format to prepare for the paper.

Asking Questions about Literature Reading

There are a number of different questions that your reading might provoke. You can explore any one of them to see how it affects your understanding of and feeling about the book. Any one of the questions could go into the response journal. Any one of them could form the basis of a paper or a project about the book. But don't think you have to include them all. Here is another one of our famous lists. It presents the kinds of questions students from around the world ask.

CHECKLIST 5.1 QUESTIONS ASKED ABOUT LITERATURE AND ITS READING

Questions about the Background of the Book
- What sort of a person is the author? How old was (s)he when the book was written?
- Where did the author come from? Does the author's race, culture, or gender tell me anything? Is the book autobiograpical?
- What is the culture or society described in the book?
- Is the book true to life? Are the time and place accurately portrayed?
- What did people think of the book when it first came out?
- How did the book happen to get published? Is there anything noteworthy about its publishing history?
- Was the book made into (or from) a film?

Questions about How the Book Is Put Together
- How is the book organized? Into parts? Chapters? Time periods? Narrators?
- Where is the major conflict in the book? Who is it between?
- What is the climax of the plot?
- Who is telling the story? What is the perspective on the events?
- Does the setting have anything to do with the organization of the book?

- Is there anything unusual or distinctive about the language in the book?
- Is it organized or patterned like any other books I have read? How would I classify it (for instance, mystery, romance, ghost story)?

Questions about Whether You Can Relate to the Book

- Does the book remind me of any incident in my life?
- Does anyone in the book remind me of someone I know?
- How did the book make me feel?
- Does the book seem true to life?
- What sort of mood did the book put me in?
- Was the book hard to put down? Why or why not?

Questions about What the Book Means or Why It Is Significant

- What does the book say about people?
- What does the book say about how people should behave?
- What does the book say about books and art or language or writing?
- Does the book have any political, religious, social, historical, or psychological significance?

Questions about Whether the Book Is Any Good

- Is it well written?
- Did it have a powerful effect?
- Is it trivial or serious?
- Was it fun to read?
- Would I recommend it to a particular sort of person?

Questions about the Book's Relation to Other Books, Films, Songs, or Plays

- Can I think of a particular book this one is like?
- Is any character like someone in another book?
- Does any part of it remind me of a folktale, myth, or similar kind of story?
- Are there any scenes that remind me of scenes in something else I've read or seen?
- Are there any words or phrases that seem familiar or that come from some source I know like the *Bible* or Greek mythology?

Most of these questions do not have a "right" answer. They are the sorts of questions that people have different answers to or different opinions about. To answer some of them (particularly those in the first group) you might have to go to an outside source, like a history book or a biography. For others you can go to a source like the editor's introduction, the anthology questions, *Cliff's Notes,* or *Masterplots* to get some idea of what other people think or have thought. If you use these sources, however, you will need to add your own opinion. In fact, if you go to these sources too early—that is, before you have had a chance to think on your own—you may have trouble finding your own opinion. Remember, secondary sources don't have a corner on the truth about the book.

Approaches to Formal Papers

Thus far, we've focused on the informal or preliminary writing you might do in literature study. Eventually, however, your instructor may ask you to write some sort of formal paper, either a "critical" paper or a research paper about a piece of literature. If the teacher sets the topic, look at Checklist 5.1 and see if you can figure out which group the assignment falls into. That can help you shape your paper.

Historical, Cultural, or Biographical Approaches. If the question you choose as the foundation for your paper deals with the background of the book, you will need to find a reference work that can help you find the answer. The reference book will probably give you information about the author, the culture, the background, or the history of the book, but it will be up to you to make a connection between what you have found out and your understanding of the book. You should prepare your essay around the underlying question, "Why is it important to know this?"

Formalist Approach. If it is a question about how the book is put together, you will need to analyze the structure, tone, or language of the book and then explain how this helps people understand or appreciate the book. It may be that the organization or the language is fun to figure out and piece together or that you used this as a clue to getting some meaning out of the book.

Reader-Response Approach. If it is a question about whether you can or how you do personally relate to the book, you will need to be detailed about the reasons why you are able—or unable—to connect with the book and specify where and how the connections are made or broken. You may explore whether the problem exists in the book or in you.

Interpretive or Philosophical Approach. If it is a question about what the book means or why it is significant, you will probably need to start by summarizing what the book is about or what the major conflict in the book might be. Then you will need to show (a) how the theme or plot is related to some larger idea like the struggle of a person to find her identity, or (b) how it reflects on our society. You will need to decide whether the book simply portrays the world or implies some sort of a comment about the world. How can you tell whether any comment is being made by the author as opposed to by one of the characters?

Evaluative Approach. If it is a question about whether the book is any good, you will need to establish your own criteria for a "good" book and then show, point by point, how the book meets or does not meet those criteria. It may be that the book is good in one way but deficient in another. For example, it may be well written but not very significant or relevant.

Comparative Approach. If it is a question about the books' relation to other books, films, songs, or plays, you will need to follow the general rules for comparison and contrast writing. You should find the specific similarities and differences, and you will probably need to quote from the two or more pieces you are relating. You may want to conclude whether the similarity makes the book more interesting to read, or whether it is simply another example of the same dull old stuff. This approach would probably focus on the particular work you are concentrating on, but could be evenly balanced between two (or among three) works.

It is possible that you will write a paper in which you answer two of these questions, or maybe even three. In that case you will need to create a general statement that shows the relationship of the parts. One example might be: This book is organized according to the typical boy-meets-girl, boy-nearly-loses-girl, boy-gets-girl framework of a love story, **but** the author takes this simple idea and makes a fascinating story because of the way she creates characters a reader can really relate to. The "hook" in this paper is going to be in the "but." You will have to show how the second part is a stronger reason for saying the book is good than the trite plot is for saying it is bad.

Picking a Question and Developing It

Let's suppose you had to write an in-class paper about the following story and were not given much more instruction than that. One way to begin is to read the story and then ask yourself, "What is the one question I want to ask about this story?"

The Sea

Poor boy. He had very big ears, and when he would turn his back to the window they would become scarlet. Poor boy. He was bent over, yellow. The man who cured came by behind his glasses. "The sea," he said, "the sea, the sea." Everyone began to pack suitcases and speak of the sea. They were in a great hurry.

The boy figured that the sea was like being inside a tremendous seashell full of echoes and chants and voices that would call from afar with a long echo. He thought that the sea was tall and green, but when he arrived at the sea, he stood still. His skin, how strange it was there. "Mother," he said because he felt ashamed, "I want to see how high the sea will come on me." He who thought that the sea was tall and green, saw it white like the head of a beer— tickling him, cold on the tips of his toes.

"I am going to see how far the sea will come on me." And he walked, he walked, he walked and the sea, what a strange thing!—grew and became blue, violet. It came up to his knees. Then to his waist, to his chest, to his lips, to his eyes. Then into his ears there came a long echo and the voices that call from afar. And in his eyes all the color. Ah, yes, at last the sea was true. It was one great, immense seashell. The sea truly was tall and green.
But those on the shore didn't understand anything about anything. Above they began to cry and scream and were saying "What a pity, Lord, what a great pity." (From *Los Niños Tontos* by Anna Maria Matute.)

Some of the questions that other students asked follow:

Who is telling the story? One student's paper showed that there is a third-person narrator who appears to be inside everyone's head, and who comments in the line "But those on the shore didn't understand anything about anything."

How do the colors help me understand the story? The paper pointed out that the colors went from yellow through the whole spectrum, but not in order. The shore encompassed the "hot" colors, and the sea the "cool" colors. This contrast then suggested that the boy was feverish and died trying to cure himself.

Does it all happen in the boy's mind? The person who wrote a paper based on this question suggested that the narrator was not an external omniscient narrator but the boy himself, who was feeling sorry for himself and that the whole story was a childish "I'll get sick and die and then everyone will feel sorry for me" sort of story.

Why is it called "The Sea" and not "The Sick Boy"? The author of a paper based on this question argued that although the central character was the boy, the sea is the central image in the story and that it must therefore be more significant than it appears. The student went on to argue that the sea is sometimes the symbol of life, and that the boy was entering into a fuller life than his family thought he could have and that they thought he was dead. What is death to some people is life to others, the writer suggested, and mentioned people going into monasteries and convents as an example.

Are we supposed to be on the boy's side? Another student considered this question by contrasting the view of the narrator at the beginning, the boy, and the people at the end. Answering the question raised another question about whether the boy was sympathetic or pitiful and stupid. The writer concluded that the author was saying that children cannot be judged the same way we judge adults.

How do we get from "Poor boy" to "what a great pity"? A fifth student writer traced the way in which we see the boy first from the outside, then into his head, first when the author uses the sentence, "The man who cured came by behind his glasses." Then we see the trip to the sea through the boy's head and stay there until the last paragraph, when we shift focus. The writer then argued that the shift in and out of the boy's head leads us to sympathize with him and also to establish a contrast that makes the story one about two ways of seeing the same event.

An answer to any one of these questions could be developed for about two pages, the amount of space that an in-class assignment might take. It wasn't choosing the right question that made the papers successful; it was choosing a question that needed a somewhat detailed answer and some proof to back up the answer. There are no "right" questions in writing about literature, there are only questions that are interesting to figure out. When you select a question, make sure it is one you want to spend some time with.

When you have selected the question and go about writing your paper, whether it is a long one or a short one, you should follow the steps we have described in Chapter 3. That is, you should work on elaborating the question or the topic. Check to see what information you need to support what you are going to say. Look for any additional sources you might need such as biographies, geographies, or histories. Get your materials arranged in front of you and begin to outline or draft what you are going to write.

We've suggested a number of ways to write about literature. The examples that follow are student papers that illustrate different levels of formality and different approaches to writing about works of literature.

Example 5.4 is a personal response to a work, a short story called "The Eclipse," by Augusto Monterroso. This response was developed from a reading log.

EXAMPLE 5.4 PERSONAL RESPONSE TO SHORT STORY

For the story "The Eclipse," I am using the phenomenological approach to give my opinion about the story.

The key feature of the text that strikes me is the fact that he is stuck out in the middle of the jungle thinking he will die; he figures how to con the natives but it backfires in his face. I really did not feel sorry for this man. He thought he was of a higher class than the natives, but as it turned out they outsmarted him by killing him.

One issue that is foregrounded is, Brother Bartolome Arrayola felt he was very important and that everybody was below him. The values implied are that the Guatemalan jungle is uncivilized and that Spain is the center of culture. I feel that it is not uncivilized it is just a little different than ours.

My viewpoint really did not change throughout the work. I just felt the wonderful Brother got his just desserts.

A gap in the story we had to fill was how Bartolome was taken to the natives village and put on the altar. They say he awakened so I figured they took him while he was sleeping.

One of my personal perspectives that was modified is that you should never underestimate people because they just might surprise you.

—Jennifer Herrick

The second example (Example 5.5) is more formal. It is an interpretation of the Keats sonnet, "When I Have Fears That I May Cease to Be."

EXAMPLE 5.5 INTERPRETING A SONNET

"When I have fears that I may cease to be"

The character in this work seems very self-conscious and fearful. He seems consumed with his own inhibitions.

The words "when" seem to be a foreground to what will happen, or the preface to his explanation of his feelings. Nothing is tied together until "-then . . ." Thoughts may be brought to a climax by the final explanation of his feelings, however, the work, by no means, is concluded. The conflicts that occur between the character and himself are not over or ended merely with the end of the work. The character still lives and has the same (and more) continual fears.

This work can be interpreted in many ways. The way I saw it was that he was scared he wouldn't accomplish all he wants to before he "ceases to be." He is afraid of many things. He is afraid that he won't love or be loved before he dies. He is scared of the world, of rejection. When he says in lines 8–9, "And think that I will never live to trace, their shadows with the magic hand of chance; . . ." to me, this explains that he fears he will never experience some things in his life. He has to fantasize about what he doesn't have.

You could also see this in another way. Maybe this work is about a man who fears that his lover is dying or is leaving him, ". . . I shall never look upon thee more," This could show his insecurities about not only his writing (books), but about love. Or is he speaking of loving someone and them not know-ing of him? ". . . of unreflecting love . . ." To me, this line is saying he fears he will never have his love reciprocated. When he says ". . . then on the share of the world I stand alone . . ." he seems to be scared of losing something dear to him, then he will be left in the world with nothing.

The last line demonstrates his true feelings, ". . . till love and fame to nothingness do sink." This says that from love and fame, he has never experienced. He then has neither and sinks into nothingness. His fears and inhibitions are evident throughout the work, but they do not conclude when the work ends—his fears remain constant in his mind. He will always be in some sort of mental conflict, he will always be in fear of not attaining all he wants before he "ceases to be."

—Nora Sanson

Example 5.6 applies a sociological model, one adapted from the theories of sociologist Milton Rokeach, to the Ibsen play *A Doll's House*. Terms such as "terminal value" and "instrumental value" are used to describe characters' motives and actions.

EXAMPLE 5.6 DESCRIBING CHARACTERS VIA
A SOCIOLOGICAL MODEL

A Doll's House: Rokeach model

Nora Helmer is the main character of the play. She experiences many conflicts. The whole play is a maturation process for her. The conflicts help her become an adult. The two conflicts that were the most pivotal in helping Nora grow up are when she was exposed to new information by Mr. Krogstad, that was inconsistent with information already present within her value system, and when she discovered existing inconsistencies within her value system.

Nora knew she had broken the law, but she believed that it was justified, "Is a daughter not to be allowed to spare her husband anxiety and care? Is a wife not to be allowed to save her husband's life? I don't know much about law but I am certain that there must be laws permitting such things as that," Nora forged the check because her terminal value of family security led her to that decision. She tried to make the right decision but Torvald and her father never allowed her to take part in the decision making process. Nora had no experience making responsible decisions. She is very much like a child, in that respect, and Torvald and her father kept her that way. Nora states, " . . . our home has been nothing but a playroom. I have been your doll-wife, just as at home I was papa's doll-child; and here the children have been my dolls. I thought it was great fun when you played with me, just as they thought it was great fun when I played with them."

She realized how she had changed herself to fit what her father and husband wanted. Nora acted the role they gave her and thought the opinions that they had. When she was conflicted internally, she looked at all her terminal and instrumental values. She realizes that, "I have other duties just as sacred . . . Duties to myself." Being a wife and mother stops being so important to her anymore. Her instrumental value of being a reasonable human being takes precedence over her terminal value of family security. In essence, her family security value was in conflict with her equality terminal value until she found out she could not have any real family security until she was a reasonable and responsible human being.

Nora's father and husband sheltered her from the difficult decisions. The only way to truly become an adult is to feel and solve conflicts, externally and internally. Nora never had that opportunity. She did not get any practice, so when she had to think on her own, she ended up breaking the law.

Torvald chastised Nora like a child, " . . . You had not sufficient knowledge to judge of the means you used." He was angry about her forging the signature but he would not accept some of the responsibility. Torvald did not even consider educating her about right or wrong, he was ready to go on as before, making her decisions and treating her like a child. That was what finally made Nora decide that she wanted to be equal and be treated like a responsible person. When she gets her education, Nora will be a responsible person, capable of making her own decisions.

—Sarah Leonard

Making the Topic Your Own

The last group of examples (Examples 5.7–5.9) give excerpts from papers in response to an assignment to answer some questions about the nature of literature. The same questions were posed at the beginning and then the end of a class "excursion" through literature:

- What is it? What does it mean? To you? To writers and readers? To society?
- How does it mean? (What is "meaning," anyway, and where is it?)
- What is it for? Who is it for?
- When it's good, what makes it good? What do you like about it? Why do you care? (Do you care?)

As you read the excerpts from the papers, you will see that the three writers start in different ways: the first with an expanded definition; the second with a list of what literature is for; and the third with an explanation of what the student plans to do and the works he'll use to illustrate his views.

EXAMPLE 5.7 "WHAT IS LITERATURE"—
BEGINNING A PAPER BY DEFINING

After reading all the selections given out in the "What is Literature?" I saw the questions listing on top of the sheet in a new light. The reading selections made me see how vague the term "Literature" is when considered. That word may have more meanings than any other word in the English language. Webster's limits its definitions to just two, but I think that there are roughly four billion different definitions, one for every man, woman, and child on the face of the earth.

I think that literature is about telling a story. Every piece of work termed as literature is trying to say something. Length has nothing to do with the meaning, a single word may contain pages of response. For example, take five minutes and write everything that comes to you about the word, "spring."

No, don't actually start writing about spring, just think of how much you have to say on the topic. A novel with 250 pages may, however, mean nothing to the same person and that is the single most important thing about literature. That's that everyone has a different interpretation of a single piece of literature and some people do not have a meaning for all pieces of literature. I will leave you with this thought, Literature means something to everyone, but can also mean nothing to someone.

—Austin Willoughby

EXAMPLE 5.8 "WHAT IS LITERATURE?"—BEGINNING BY LISTING

Before starting this paper I reviewed the questions and my answers to "What is Literature." I found that very little did my answers change. I still think that literature is any piece of writing, from books to poems, or things that people write themselves. Literature is for entertainment and it can inspire you or turn you away from something. It can teach you things and help you share your feelings and experiences. You can write literature to get your anger out, to re-capture a special event in your life, or to just be creative.

—Amy Lemp

EXAMPLE 5.9 "WHAT IS LITERATURE?"—
BEGINNING BY GIVING A PLAN

For my "So what?" paper, I will answer the questions about literature and explain how my answers have changed since I first answered them. The works which I have chosen to write about include; "Gretel in Darkness," "Not Waving but Drowning," "The Writer," and three other works of interest. This project about literature has opened my mind and has made my interest in literature more intense. I enjoyed many of the works, and six of these I will write about.

—Darin Bowerman

These last three examples suggest that in writing about literature, as in writing about many other topics, one of the things you must do is figure out a way to make the topic your own; then you can write a paper that will show your investment in the topic and the way it is written.

We have a few miscellaneous pieces of advice for writing about literature that we summarize in Checklist 5.2.

CHECKLIST 5.2 SUGGESTIONS FOR WRITING ABOUT LITERATURE

- Use text references to show the connections between the work and your conclusions or assertions of meaning. Direct quotes are best. But don't let the quote just sit there; make sure your reader knows what to look for in it.

- Be sure to include the title and author of the work(s) you are discussing in the first paragraph of your paper.

- Assume that your reader has read the book but does not have detailed recall of it and doesn't have the book at hand.

- Avoid going line by line or chapter by chapter or you will be sure to end up with a dull paraphrase.

- Avoid the following expressions:

  What the author wanted to say . . . You only know what the author wrote.

  The hidden meaning of the story is . . . If it's hidden, how do you know what it is?

  An interesting part of the book is . . . It probably won't be interesting to your reader.

*In Jane Smith's novel **The Earthworm**, she tells* . . . the "she" isn't clearly Jane Smith. Make it *In **The Earthworm**, Jane Smith tells* . . .

This symbol represents . . . A symbol catalog isn't wanted. What's wanted is what you make of it and how you use a symbol.

- Avoid words or phrases like *cute, funny, smooth, imaginative, deep,* or *meaningful.* These need to have examples to show what you mean and they are such absolutes that people will be set up to disagree.

Literature-Related Projects

In addition to writing papers about literature, there are a number of projects that you and the class might undertake. Some of them can be put directly into your portfolio, but some might require additional work.

Discussion. Probably one of the things that you will spend a lot of class time on is talking about the reading you have done, either in small groups or as a whole class. How do you know whether it's been a good discussion? Normally people can tell because they want to keep on talking, or because everyone takes part, or because the questions that have been raised are ones that are hard to answer and send people off to the library or back to rereading the book. The problem with most discussions is that when it's been a good one, people have been so involved, they haven't had a chance to take notes or turn on a tape recorder.

During a discussion, keep a pad or a notebook handy so that you can jot down important points. You can also write them in the book itself. You probably have your own note-taking technique. Then the best thing to do after a good discussion is to write it up in your response journal and make sure that some of the others have also written up something in their logs or journals. Then you can write up a summary of the points that have been raised. One way to do this is to use the following format:

Discussion Record

Date:
Participants:
Book Discussed:

Main Points Raised: By Whom:
1.
2.
3.
Conclusions and next steps:
Evaluation:

This form can then be inserted in the portfolios of each of the participants. You can also ask the instructor to include an evaluation if she or he
was present at the discussion.

Performance. In many cases, particularly with plays and poetry, you may
make a performance of the work. You might do reader's theater in which
you and some other students present the text formally (without memoriz-
ing it or using gestures and actions other than your voices). You might do
an oral interpretation of a poem as a solo or with other voices if it seems
appropriate. You might even do a full-scale performance on the stage. In
that case, you may have an audiotape or videotape of the performance
that can be put in the portfolio, but it should be accompanied by a
statement about what you did, why you did it, and what you learned from
what you did. This is the main writing task you will have to undertake,
and it should carry the argument about you that the tape supports.

Let's say your class did an enactment of *Raisin in the Sun*, and instead of
just sitting in chairs and reading the parts, you stood up, moved around
and enacted a scene or two. Some of you took some additional time in
rehearsing and presenting it and one of you videotaped the performance.
The performance seemed successful, and when you looked at the tape as a
class, you decided you liked it. You could copy the tape for each portfolio,
but you should also have some sort of a written self-assessment of your
participation.

Be sure to say something about what specific part you played in the
production, when it took place, what you learned about the play from
having taken part in the production, and what you learned about the craft
of the theatre or the art of being a camera person. Also be sure to explain
the important decisions you made about movement, tone, pace, angle, and
everything else that went into your production. This self-evaluation can
go with the tape.

Translation. We don't mean translating from one language to another as in
English to Spanish, but translating from one medium to another or adapting the piece of literature to modern times. Some people draw well and
will illustrate a story or a poem. Some may take a poem and set it to music.
Some make a game out of a book they have read. Each of these is a kind of
translation.

In one of our classes, the students translated Shakespeare's *Julius Caesar* into modern times. There were five groups, each of which took an act; the group with Act I turned it into a rap; those with Act II set the conspiracy on campus; those with Act III placed it in Congress, those with Act IV filmed the action up in the hills, and those with Act V did it with a voice-over. In each case, the group presented their work in class either with a videotape or a live performance that was then videotaped.

The students who included this work in their portfolio also wrote an explanation of why they did what they did to translate the act, what decisions they had to make, what part they took in the group work, and whether they thought it was successful or not.

COMPUTERS AT WORK:
Using Technology with Literature

There are an increasing number of computer programs dealing with literature. Many of these include CD ROM so that people can move from text to picture to video. You may not have the equipment to do this sort of fancy work with a piece of literature. But there are some simpler activities.

You can build a computer file of the class's interpretations of a novel so that each student can go into the file, find out what another person thinks is important and evaluate the comment or make a different comment. Then, as a final project, these can be assembled and edited into a master document.

This group file can be done with a hypertext program so that there will be different files for the various main topics, background, history, critical interpretations, personal responses, and other comments. In some courses, the file is added to over the years.

Some students have taken a selection and created a computer game out of it. *Macbeth* makes a good game on the order of *Where in the World is Carmen Sandiego*.

If the class has a modem and communications software, there can be correspondence about a novel across campuses. In fact, there now exist poetry workshops on the main networks so that students around the world can share poems and criticisms.

Computer graphics may be a good way to enhance the text you are working on. Illustrations together with commentary can make a good critical paper.

Chapter Summary

In this chapter you have seen how there may be many topics to write about in a literature course and how you can generate them from a response journal.

You have gone through the ways by which some students develop questions into papers.

You have looked at some of the ways in which other kinds of activities with literature can be turned into material for your portfolio.

We now move into the second part of the book, the part that explores ways to revise your writing to make it work for you and ways to present the final paper and the portfolio. Some people say that the easy part is over, now the hard part begins. But if you have begun well, the revision should not be a serious problem.

6 Revision

Do You Know:

- How to read your own paper for purpose, direction, and content?
- What to look for when revising paragraphs and sentences?
- How to revise a paper to serve a particular purpose in your portfolio?
- How to use a computer to store and revise several works for your portfolio?

Looking Ahead

You have seen how different kinds of writing assignments might get planned and drafted. Now we are going to explore the art of revision, taking your first draft and looking at it critically to see how it can be improved. We will explain how to look at the whole and then at the various parts: paragraphs, sentences, and words. We will discuss how to benefit from the input of others and how to use technology to make the process easier to handle.

riting is a process that involves more than just composing. If composing whatever you have to write is Part I, revision is Part II. Often neglected or done carelessly, revision is the step that can break or, done well, make your effort. However, the biggest challenge to face in Part II is in the very same place as in Part I—getting started. Although it's hard to do, we all must face revision before we finish with a piece. For instance, this book underwent several revisions—some small, some major—before it was printed. Part of what we did was adding, part changing, part throwing away. How a writer approaches this critical step can determine the quality of the final product.

We all have our own methods of writing. Because revision is a critical part of the writing process, we also may have different styles of approaching it. But some suggestions hold true whether we revise the piece as a whole at once, do it piece by piece as we go along, or do a little of both.

If you use a computer or word processor and compose directly on the screen, your instructor may ask you to print your work at some specific point in time. This document can be referred to as a first draft even though you have spent time reworking parts of it while composing. Regardless of how that draft is identified, you need to pause in the process and read what you have written from beginning to end, without interrupting yourself or giving in to minor distractions. This dedicated read-through reorients you to your entire writing and makes you experience what your reader will experience. During this read-through, you should keep several questions in mind, but do not stop to answer them until you have finished reading your work through at least once. Above all, keep in mind:

- the purpose for which you are writing,
- the main point you wish to make, and
- the needs of the audience you want to reach.

Communication Is the Point

These issues are basic to communicating in an appropriate way with your audience, and, after all, communication is the point. Although some writing is for your benefit alone, once you prepare for a publication of any type (by handing in a paper, submitting it to a newspaper or magazine, sending it to a friend or stranger, or including it in your presentation or cumulative portfolio), you must begin to account for the needs of your audience, which stand equal to yours at this point.

After your first read-through, you should be able to turn early considerations into questions and answer them with a sentence or two. Ask yourself:

- Is my purpose in writing this work clear?
- Have I identified my main point?
- Have I helped my audience understand my purpose and my point?

Make sure you draw conclusions about your work from exactly what you have read in that particular piece of writing and nothing else. Try not to excuse yourself by thinking that because you knew the background or reason for something, therefore others will also. Being honest with yourself about your work is very hard, but is another skill good writers work to develop.

Working with Peers

To guard against being too hard or too easy with yourself, ask someone else to serve as an editor. Every classroom has many resources in it, and the other people are the most important ones. The people in your class or course help in major ways. First, they can serve as your first audience outside yourself and provide you with an opportunity for face-to-face discussion of the ideas in your paper. Next, working with another person forces you to be clear and specific about your meaning before you take a grading risk. In addition, you can share in the group knowledge about correct expression. Even professional writers have editors who inevitably catch careless errors left after umpteen drafts have been reviewed by the author.

When you ask someone to serve as your partner, it is best at that stage to tell that person your reason for sharing your work. Have your reader answer the same questions you posed for your read-through. If the two sets of answers agree with each other and with what you intended, congratulations! You have just a little "clean up" work to get the copy ready. (More on that later.) However, if the answers turn out to be other than what you expected, you need to make a new plan.

You can use a first-draft evaluation form (see Figure 6.1) with a partner to get you started. The form is useful in many assignments. You can fill in the "Style Concerns" and "Editing Concerns" sections when your group or class discusses the rubric or evaluation criteria with the teacher. This will also help focus the discussion between you and your partner, helping both of you stay on target and concentrate on the paper and assignment.

Once again, different people approach this step in different ways, but taking a look at the many concerns that come up in revision is helpful. If you remember that communicating is the purpose of most public writing, you will find yourself concentrating your efforts on clarifying your ideas for others. Focus on that broad task first.

FIGURE 6.1 FIRST-DRAFT EVALUATION FORM

ELEMENTS OF REVISION

NAME OF AUTHOR: _____ **PARTNER:** _____

TITLE OF PAPER: _____ **DATE:** _____

(You must have one of these sheets completed for each assignment in this unit. Notice, please, that **another person** must help complete your review.)

1. **Revising Partner:** What is the main point of this paper? Please write a short statement of your understanding of this:

   _____

   _____

Author: Please read the above. If it does not match your intention in a general way, please list the steps you must take to make your point more clearly. Follow those steps and begin the process anew.

After clarifying your main point to your satisfaction, proceed with the rest of the evaluation as outlined. Respond to each of the questions in writing and clip to paper.

2. Have you chosen vocabulary and sentence structure suited to the purpose of the paper? Suited to the intended audience of the paper?

List examples:

3. Are your examples or support clear? Suited to the purpose? Familiar or explained to the audience?

Best one:

4. Is each paragraph unified? Detail here the process you followed to check.

5. Style Concerns (Task specific):

   A.

   B.

5. Editing Concerns (Task specific):

   A.

   B.

Grading Point: Describe it here: _____

Clarify Ideas

First, identify the part (or parts) of your paper that causes the most confusion and reexamine its elements. Using checklists sometimes helps (see Chapters 3 and 7). Perhaps your teacher has a list you feel comfortable with, or maybe you have developed one of your own that helps you focus on important characteristics.

Whatever resource you use to help you, look at what you have written with a critical eye, taking the role of an outsider to the thinking process behind the paper. Line up the checklist side by side with your paper and concentrate on one question at a time, reading and rereading your writing to find the answers to all the checklist questions you think are important.

Next, rewrite each of the problematic sections and recheck them. Read them in the context of the whole paper, making sure the revised part "fits" in the progression of ideas and the style of the rest of the paper. Each time you do this, you should read the entire paper again.

C O M P U T E R S   A T   W O R K :

Saving Drafts

If you use a computer to write your papers, do not delete the old material before you have replaced the ideas in the new section. To save a record of the first effort and to avoid cluttering your screen with material to be discarded as well as new composition, make sure you print hard copy. If you decide at a later time that you preferred the original, you still have a copy of it. Keeping a hard copy of first drafts will also help you build a record of your writing process for possible inclusion in your portfolio.

Think about Purpose

Why are you writing? The simple answer—because it was assigned—helps only a little in the revising process. If that's the best answer you have, though, it still raises questions about the writing.

▲▲▲▲▲▲▲▲▲▲▲▲▲▲▲▲▲▲▲▲▲▲▲▲▲▲▲▲▲▲▲▲▲▲▲▲

THINKING ABOUT . . .

Purpose

Ask Yourself:

- Have I answered the question the assignment posed?
- Is it the right length? Is it in the assigned format?
- Does the material show what I know about the assignment's topic?
- Is the information in it clear? Is it the best kind to serve the purpose of the paper? Does it include any special information that might be specific to this assignment or class?
- Is it written in the "language" expected in the class?

The last two questions especially concern writing for courses and purposes other than English or composition courses. Remember, although some people on some occasions write for the joy of it and to share discovery of art, the world, or themselves, much of the purpose of writing in school or college is to communicate with others what you know about something—the consequences of World War I, the results of a laboratory investigation, the mathematical process you followed to arrive at an answer, the characteristics of a particular artist, a plan for compiling data on your town's oral history. In these situations, there are subject-specific vocabularies that make expression easier and demonstrate your command over the subject.

In addition, for some subjects, professionals in the field may have developed a particular style of writing that is now used consistently. After you read textbooks or articles written by such people, you begin to get the idea. Using subject-specific tools or styles is not perceived as imitation for its own sake, but as an indication that you are aware of the demands of the subject and are practicing its skills.

As you revise, think of the process as an inverted pyramid (see Figure 6.2). Begin with the major ideas, including the reason you have written your paper, the point you want to make. After you have verified that overall the paper presents your major idea well (and fits the assignment, if that's an element), look at smaller contributing ideas and their construction at the paragraph level. Next, review sentence construction and effectiveness. Finally, check individual words for appropriateness.

FIGURE 6.2 THE REVISING PROCESS

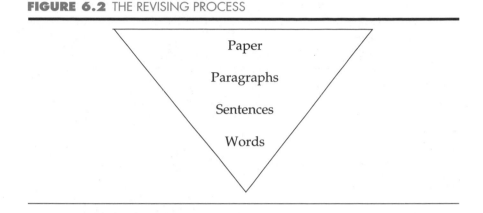

Think about the Main Point

The main point is the single most important thought you want to share. As an exercise, or as part of a response form, your first editor should be able to state the main point of your paper and this statement should correspond to your intention. It may not be exactly the same because each reader brings something different to a paper, but it should be a reasonable approximation of your idea.

Of course, the easiest way to guarantee that a reader will be able to identify your point is to tell her directly, à la "I am writing about . . ." However, this technique leaves a bit to be desired stylistically in most formats. With the wide range of possible purposes for writing, it is not possible to construct a single rule to govern how to communicate your main point. Some considerations based on your purpose in writing might help you with these decisions.

A style that is acceptable or desirable in a report would be inappropriate or boring in a fictional narrative, but both must have a main point around which the rest of the material you produce is gathered.

The shorter the paper, the more direct you must be about your point. Once again, purpose determines choice! Although you should adjust how you communicate your main point to the format, making sure that you signal your main idea and making the rest of the paper revolve around it are of prime importance.

Think about Content and Context

Consider the balance of information and form in your paper. Although this is a book about writing, we need to remind you that most school or college writing is done for a purpose other than one exclusively for practice in writing and often it is assigned by instructors other than those in the English department.

As an element in any revision process, the accuracy of the information and conclusions you have drawn about your topic must be verified. Good writing technique can help a poorly researched idea only so much. In many academic writing projects the content (what you write) is as important as the context (how you write it); and you should subject it to a revision evaluation as well. Some general suggestions can apply to several subjects.

For all statements or conclusions in your paper, is there effective support?

Is the order of ideas easy to follow and clear?

Have you used the proper format for citation, if that applies?

Think about Your Audience

Look at your writing as if it were a public performance. In all public writing, or writing outside your personal journal, some other person must be able to take meaning from the material you provide. You need to consider the needs of that potential reader.

Much of what you write at this stage of your life is course based. Occasionally, an assignment carries with it an identified audience, either real or created, as part of the assignment. Sometimes, the instructor is the only audience you can reasonably expect, but the range of possible audience is large and difficult to pinpoint. Getting a fix on the intended audience helps you adjust style and content. When you begin writing, you may have an audience in mind. It's helpful to check that again once you've written the draft. Put yourself in your audience's place as you make that read-through. Evaluate whether your target group of persons will know more about you or about your topic at the end of your paper.

For instance, if the work you are revising is an essay on an assigned topic, class requirements regarding information (amount and kind), format (what shape it's in, its length) and style (formal or informal, narrative, expository) should guide your revision efforts. The features of a letter to the editor may require a different style and a more specific focus than a short description of an imaginary place. If the original assignment was written, keep a copy of that by you as you read through.

Use Active Language

In addition to format and content considerations, audience raises the issue of language. We each have a variety of speaking and writing languages that we call upon depending on the situation. In any case, using active language, such as vivid action verbs (instead of various forms of "to be") energizes your writing and moves a reader through your ideas. As part of your technical edit, you should make an effort to vitalize verbs and standardize the tense you use throughout your paper:

Original: He gave the book to his neighbor.
Revised: handed, threw, pushed, sneaked, delivered, passed.

Original: She was friendly.
Revised: She smiled, looked me in the eyes, and shook my hand.

Original: The people got to the class late.
Revised: Arrived, sneaked in, began, ran into, crawled into.

The vocabulary you choose makes statements about you and can help or hinder your audience's understanding. It should be consistent with the purpose of your paper, but also serve your primary goal of communicating. Above all, evaluate whether the language you chose "sounds" like you. Often a feature of purpose, this language choice also involves your personal attitude toward the work and, in some cases, your teacher's, if the writing is for school.

Explain Your Ideas

In some circumstances, you cannot know the characteristics of the unseen audience, as in application essays or state or national test essays. This "unknown" audience may not already share much of the information you are writing about. Be sure to be clear and explain your ideas. Talk about and define heavy metal rock rather than simply using band names or song titles to make your point. Remembering the purpose of the activity and your goals in doing the writing should give you some suggestions about which level of language to use. In the read-through, pay attention to the general impression a reader would get and check that the language is consistent.

Checking on purpose, main idea and support, and attention to audience are considerations you use when reading through the paper as a whole. Remember to finish whatever revising task you are engaged in with a read-through of the entire paper. Once you are satisfied that the general impression the paper gives is what you want, you can move on to the smaller parts that make up the entire effect.

Even if you are pleased overall with your paper, your read-through may point out spots that are not as tight as they could be or that don't fit together well. In that case, focus next on the paragraphs, the building blocks of the paper. Each paragraph should be able to stand alone, while following up on the preceding paragraph and linking the following one.

Revising Paragraphs

Many people find that working at the paragraph level gives them the most immediate satisfaction. A paragraph is limited in topic and provides a "canvas" small enough so that efforts to polish and refine show results quickly. And tackling any major project bit by bit makes the task seem less threatening.

THINKING ABOUT . . .

Revising Paragraphs

As you read each paragraph, ask yourself about:

Unity
- Is there one topic, stated or unstated, that connects all the information?

Coherence
- Is all the information in the paragraph closely related to its topic?
- Is each sentence in the paragraph related to the topic and necessary to expand it?

Transition
- Does the beginning of the paragraph connect it to the one that comes before it?
- Have you signaled that connection with a word or sentence bridging the two?
- Have you used the final sentence to tie up the topic of the paragraph?
- Does the final sentence lead the reader to the next paragraph?

Remember: once you adjust a paragraph, you should reread the material before and after it to make sure that your revised paragraph fits into the general scheme of the paper. Do this every time you make revisions to paragraphs. Occasionally, this step in the revision process will show that a paragraph belongs somewhere else in the paper.

If you are handwriting, try not to make so many directional lines on your copy that you become confused about what goes where. If you use numbers or letters to identify paragraphs, you'll be able to avoid hand-written drafts marked with lines going every which way. Highlighting the "signpost" letters with a colored marker will draw your attention when you recopy for a final draft.

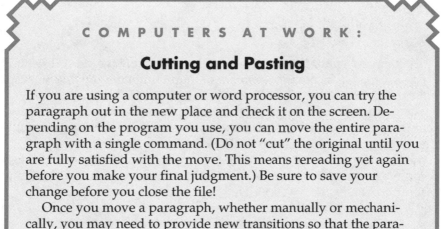

C O M P U T E R S   A T   W O R K :

Cutting and Pasting

If you are using a computer or word processor, you can try the paragraph out in the new place and check it on the screen. Depending on the program you use, you can move the entire paragraph with a single command. (Do not "cut" the original until you are fully satisfied with the move. This means rereading yet again before you make your final judgment.) Be sure to save your change before you close the file!

Once you move a paragraph, whether manually or mechanically, you may need to provide new transitions so that the paragraph fits in its new location. Scroll through the entire paper to verify that the paragraph "hooks up" with the material around it.

Revising Sentences

Having checked paragraphs, move to the glue that holds the blocks together—the sentences. Polishing sentences can make a paper flow. When you look at your sentences, think about correctness, of course, but also be aware of style. It is at the sentence level that the rhythm of your paper arises.

Incomplete Sentences

When checking for sentence completeness, your awareness of audience and the purpose of your paper should be your guide. Pay special attention to sentences beginning with subordinate clauses or phrases (like the first sentence of this paragraph). Using "because" at the beginning of a sentence is perfectly acceptable, if you remember to follow it with a main clause. Because you may not know what a main clause is, we provide this example. The same logic applies when using a verbal at the beginning of a sentence. Frequently, verbal clauses (which are incomplete sentences) will actually belong in the sentence before:

Original: Writers may miss those trailers. Editing in a hurry.

Beginning the sentence with the verbal clause solves the problem.

Revised: Editing in a hurry, writers may miss those trailers.

Phrases and subordinate clauses can involve many words and several ideas and remain incomplete sentences. Length is not the key to sentences, but coherence and completeness of ideas are key.

Caution: Although some professional authors have used incomplete sentences as stylistic devices, at this stage in your career it is not necessarily a good idea, unless you can articulate a good reason for doing so. There are certainly exceptions—dialogue comes to mind. People often do not use complete sentences in speech, so writing that imitates speech will contain incomplete sentences as well. Outside of narrative, however, you need to be very careful about completeness.

Run-on Sentences

A closely related error to incomplete sentences is the run-on sentence. Although length is a sign, it alone does not define a run-on. Once again, the test focuses on ideas. If all other methods fail, you can use the "ear" test. If a reader who is speaking takes a significant breath between ideas, consider whether those ideas should be divided into separate sentences.

Phrases and Clauses

Sentences give the paper its pace. Series of short sentences, many of them beginning with the same word (frequently "the") lulls the reader into a pattern. If that goes on long enough, the pattern, rather than the ideas, takes over the reader's impression. To address that problem, maintain an awareness of the length, variety of form, and beginnings of sentences. To vary the beginnings of sentences, you can change the order of the elements of the sentence, reversing the order of phrases or clauses. In this paragraph, most sentences begin with different words: "Sentences," "Series," "If," "To," "In." The first sentence is very short (six words) and the last will be short as well. Variety helps flow.

Other times, you may have to add a phrase or word to the beginning of a sentence to break up a pattern. Combining sentences that express ideas that are consistent with one another will help eliminate short, choppy sentences, but be conscious of providing the connection (conjunction) that fits the new meaning of the combined sentence:

> *Original: The writer edits carefully. Checking for correctness is important. It is also critical that you check for style.*

> *Revised: The careful writer edits for style and for correctness.*

Because a word processor makes this task so easy, be careful to check the connections each time you edit.

Sentences that are direct and active involve a reader in the material. Passive sentences, which often fail to identify the actor in the sentence, have their place, but should not be overused. "Paper-speak," both in and out of the academic world, often relies on passive voice and is one of the reasons so many people complain about hard-to-read reports. Make the majority of your sentences active, with the subject and the agent the same. This moves the language along. We list the few exceptional uses of the passive in the Appendix on grammar topics.

Mechanics and usage issues raise their heads during revision, although checking for them more correctly comes under editing. Always check for subject-verb agreement, pronoun-antecedent agreement, and clear reference. In addition, look at the tense of the verbs. To check tenses, a writer needs to look at the verbs in sentences. Usually, tense should be consistent throughout the paper, unless varying it serves the purpose of the paper. For instance, a short story involving a flashback will contain a larger range of tenses than a history report on an event which has been completed.

For more on grammar and style, see the Appendix.

Revising Words

Revising at the word level involves decisions about appropriateness or aptness. Depending on several features of the paper, namely, the purpose or the intended audience, the writer makes choices about vocabulary.

Although many words have synonyms of generally equivalent meaning, these separate words have different values in precision of expression, effect on the audience, or mood and tone of the piece. In these considerations, connotation is as important as denotation or definition. The shade of meanings and its feeling (the connotation) of *skinny* differs from that of *slender, slim,* or *thin.* Which would you rather be called?

Editing, the final step in preparing a paper for publication, often involves word level concerns exclusively. It is the last check out of necessity, because many revision decisions add or subtract words, move them around, or change the context.

COMPUTERS AT WORK:

On-line Thesauruses

If you are using a word processor during this process, referring to the thesaurus (if there is one) can be helpful. However, many computers used in schools have limited memories, so the range of words included in a thesaurus on the hard drive may be smaller than you need. Using a thesaurus is a good first step in expanding the word choice, but you need to check the use of a word in an expanded dictionary before you use it.

Mechanics and usage issues at the sentence level can affect the spelling of words as well. A word processor or computer program often includes a spellchecker, which generally makes the process easier. Even if you use a word processor, however, you need to check homophones or homonyms. These are words which sound alike, but differ in meaning or spelling. Example: *bear* and *bare.* The spellcheck feature will not pick these up and carelessness in this area can create a negative impression on a person who is grading your paper.

Those poor spellers among us without computer helpers need to be especially aware of this step. If spelling confuses you beyond the help of a dictionary, ask another person to act as your editor. Spelling contributes to the overall impression that your paper gives and leads to better communication.

Revising for the Portfolio

This chapter has so far explored revision issues on individual papers or projects, separate from each other. Each paper that you submit for grading or publication needs to go through that revision process. In some courses, your work taken as a whole and produced over time demonstrates your achievement in that course. In these courses, people look at several pieces of your work as evidence that you have accomplished a goal or set of goals. The choice of which papers or works to include in this portfolio depends on many factors—some decided by school authorities, some decided by your teacher, some negotiated between you and your instructor, and some chosen by you alone. We explore this topic in great detail in Chapter 8, but here we simply want to make some points as they apply to your revision of individual papers.

Courses emphasizing the evaluation of work produced over time may use the concept of portfolio as an opportunity for each student to demonstrate what he or she has learned or how she or he has progressed. Portfolios contain several examples of its creator's work, each piece selected for what it shows about the creator as a student or as an accomplished participant in a learning process. As the portfolio maker and the author of the work in it, you will make many decisions about what part of your total work product goes into the portfolio, what each piece shows about you, and how all the pieces together present a picture of your performance. Revising your work with inclusion in the portfolio in mind necessitates further steps to the process you used when you treated each paper separately.

Choosing Papers

Choosing papers for the portfolio once again must involve your consideration of audience and purpose. What does the piece show about your performance in the class? Does the particular paper demonstrate your range of ability? Does it summarize the results of a unit of study? Will it showcase a newly developed skill? Can it fill a gap in what is currently in the portfolio? Would it work better with the other papers in your portfolio than one there already?

For instance, you may want to show a range of skills in persuasive techniques. In evaluating papers you consider for the portfolio, you need to focus carefully on the elements of persuasion utilized by each paper or part of a paper. Base your critique on how effectively the writing convinces the reader both of the validity of your argument and the skillfulness of your writing.

On the surface, these may seem like the same thing, but careful reflection will show that while a piece of writing may be acceptable by itself, when you remember the special purpose of the writing to contribute to the portfolio, that paper needs to pass another "test." Not all the papers you have written in the persuasive mode may be necessary or appropriate for the portfolio. This decision depends on criteria developed in the course or on the other examples you have included in the portfolio. Those are decisions independent of whether an individual paper, by itself, is finished or not.

Reflecting on Your Writing

Before you include any paper in the portfolio, you need to articulate the reason(s) for that decision. Some portfolio systems will provide a short form for you to detail the elements of the paper that you have chosen, and we show some approaches in Chapter 8. In other systems, the writer needs to write a reflection about her pieces of work and what each shows about her skills.

These reflective writings also become a part of the portfolio, but to provide framework for the other work, not necessarily to be judged as part of the body of work as well. They glue the pieces together into a unified whole and provide a reviewer signposts for her reading of the portfolio. It helps that person to stay on track and may clear up connections between pieces of writing.

If you want the portfolio reader to see how well you handle contrasts of character in your paper, tell the reader to look at papers A and D for that reason. Don't make the reader guess—he or she may come to conclusions you don't want! A creator of a portfolio needs to remember to make clear to this "outsider" why he or she has chosen the particular pieces that are in the portfolio. The reviewer becomes one of the many audiences a writer must consider.

Meeting Instructor Criteria

In checking over your portfolio, you may discover that it is lacking papers to demonstrate a particular characteristic that you think is important about you or that your teacher has told you to show. Some teachers distribute their guidelines for evaluating student portfolios at the beginning of the class or semester. These may include, but are not limited to, looking for evidence of students': personal voice, use of the writing process, range of command of style, content knowledge for a unit, ability to compose in various formats, growth as a writer and communicator, and flexibility with different conditions (time, length, individual, group).

Before you consider your portfolio complete, make sure you have samples which meet all the criteria that have been identified as important.

As you review your work over time, you may find that you have some papers that partially fit the need the portfolio has generated, but that, while acceptable as assignments when they were written, need further work to satisfy the range you want your portfolio to show. Reworking and revising a paper written for another reason, with this new purpose in mind, can fulfill the portfolio requirements while giving you more practice in revision for a specific purpose. You may even note that third or fourth effort in the explanation which accompanies the piece in the portfolio.

If you find there are missing sections in your treatment of a topic, you have another opportunity to revise an already existing piece or write a new piece to fit the need. Portfolio evaluation gives you an opportunity to take an overall approach to your learning and a chance to demonstrate in a deliberate way what you know about a topic.

When summarizing the results of a unit of work in any class, papers written separately in response to specific assignments may not show your grasp or accomplishment in the unit of study. Perhaps you have chosen assignments that do not cover all the skills or knowledge involved in the unit, or perhaps what you have written for one part of the unit was less than satisfactory. How many times have you thought that "if you knew then what you know now . . ."? Sometimes instructors agree and are interested in the change that may result from just a little more effort or knowledge. Portfolio evaluation allows you another chance to review your work on that topic as a whole, assessing each piece in relation to the entire unit, rather than a stand-alone demonstration.

Adapting Graded Papers for New Uses

When you think that something you've already been graded on can be adapted to a new use in the portfolio, check with the person who has graded the paper or, if you know who it is, will evaluate the portfolio. He or she may have suggestions, provide another perspective, or suggest that your efforts would be better spent on something else. If you do pursue the revision on the paper, make sure you account for the changes that you make. Include your reasoning for the "second look" and provide some record of the decisions for the revision. Explain:

- Why did the original need the change?
- What steps did you follow to change the original?
- How does the new and improved version fit into the portfolio better than the former?

These self-evaluations are an important part of the portfolio picture of you as a deliberate writer. Showing that you know why as well as how you choose pieces for assessment or demonstration contributes to the overall image of you that an evaluator will see.

In addition to the explanations for including the revised paper, you may want to retain the original version of the paper in the portfolio as well. Many people, including assessors, critics, and other writers, are interested in tracking the process a writer goes through in revision. Editions separated by time and perspective can show important growth. Make sure you point out the effect that your changes have made on the specific paper and include an explanation of how this set of papers adds to the portfolio picture of you as a writer and a learner.

Revision of any type, whether it is revision of individual papers or revision for the portfolio, requires that the writer take an objective look at work he or she has done. Having a plan to guide this effort will help you overcome the feelings you may have about your own creations and gives a specific purpose to your critique. Remembering the purpose of your revision, featuring the main point of your paper, and focusing on the needs of the audience the writing is intended for provide direction for the time and effort demanded by revision.

Chapter Summary

To revise effectively, you must be able to read from beginning to end with your revising purpose in mind. After you reread your work for purpose, you need to check direction, content, and audience needs.

The next steps are evaluating paragraphs and sentences, and then on to such word-level concerns as grammar, mechanics, usage, and other conventions. Knowing typical connections between form and function is useful, as is knowing the conventional ways of reporting things and giving signals in the text.

Revising the paper to hand in the first time is one part of revision. You also have a chance to revise the paper for your portfolio. Here is a time when you can look over the particular piece in light of all your writing and see what it says about you as a writer. You may also change it again if it makes sense to do so.

7 Turning Your Paper into a Final Product

Looking Ahead

The preceding chapters have brought us to the point of making finished products or final drafts. In this chapter, you'll see steps to follow to select the best draft, judge your own work, do final editing, and format and print the paper. As always, you will make many decisions. And, again, there are many evaluation questions to help you make that last look at your paper before someone else judges it.

You have written your draft, gone over it, and revised it; you think it is now ready to hand in. It probably is, but there are some last steps to take so you can get it ready for whoever is going to judge it. This stage is where you have to act more as an editor and publisher—and less as a writer. After all, your paper is being launched to a new audience, one that hasn't seen it before, one that will judge it (and you, too) by what they see, not by what you tell them.

The Production Stage

In the world of professional writing, production time is often longer than writing time. This was particularly true long ago, when a copyist would take a draft and write it out in a neat, legible style. Any blot and the page had to be started over again. It was a little better when type was set by hand, with a person putting the pages together letter by letter in a frame and then printing the text page by page. When typewriters came along, things were able to go a little faster, but before the invention of white correction fluid and the copying machine, a page would still have to be retyped if there was an error. With word-processing programs and laser printers, the production stage can be speeded up, but a number of checks still have to be done so as to have the text in its absolutely positively final form. In this chapter we will assume that you have a typewriter or a word processor and we will not create a special section on computers. What we say applies to nearly any technology you might use.

Lets return to your revised draft. When you are satisfied with it, you can then begin what we call the production stage. In most cases, that stage involves these steps:

- selecting your best draft;
- editing;
- formatting, including using graphics;
- printing and copying; and
- keeping process notes.

Selecting Your Best Draft

Selecting your best draft, the first step, is actually part of the revising we discussed in the last chapter, but it is possible that you have kept a number of versions of your paper, either in what is known as hard copy or as different files on your computer disk. You should clearly label or date each of these so you know which one is the latest version. This is probably the one that you like the best. We do not recommend that you throw out the other drafts; too many horror stories about lost copies and files advise against saving just one copy of what you have done.

Let's assume that you have made your final revision (it is actually the next-to-final one). Look briefly at the earlier versions of what you wrote to see if there is anything that you threw away that now looks good. It may be that you took out an example because it looked as if you had too many. Should it go back in? Is the one you removed a better example than the one you kept? If you are not sure, show the paper to someone else. Perhaps your writing partner or your instructor can help you decide.

Another approach is to look at your instructor's comments on the drafts you have already turned in. These can give you a clue as to whether the current version of your writing is doing what you want.

A Digression on Grading and Marks

As you think about the best version and go into production, you should remember that your paper is going to be read and marked or graded by your instructor. We think you should be aware of their concerns, which are similar to the concerns of most readers in the world. About as many grading systems exist as instructors to apply them. Some instructors carefully mark each little error in red; some simply put a letter grade on the top of the paper; others write responses instead of grades. We have reviewed some of the research on how instructors mark and on the kinds of comments they make about papers.

Instructors may or may not mark a particular grammatical lapse or spelling mistake; they may or may not use a phrase like *awk* or *stc frg*; they may or may not occasionally write *good* or *interesting* in the margin. Usually, however, they do make some kind of summary comment. We have collected and defined the adjectives they tend to use when they are praising a composition (more often than not, they use the opposites of these adjectives), and what they mean by them. It is a good practice for students to use these terms and ask each other which ones apply to the papers they are working on.

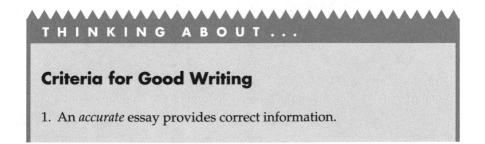

THINKING ABOUT . . .

Criteria for Good Writing

1. An *accurate* essay provides correct information.

2. An *appealing* essay is enjoyable to read, able to evoke a certain atmosphere, and/or appeal to the senses and emotions successfully.

3. A *effective* essay is eloquent, vivid, and emphatic in providing a convincing, arresting argument or description that makes the writer's point.

4. An *original* treatment of the topic is inspired and imaginative, possessing a freshness of feeling. It interests and stimulates the reader.

5. A *concisely* written composition tells the maximum amount in a minimum of words. Its simple, straight-to-the-point style captures the essential ideas efficiently.

6. A composition is *well connected* when there are clear transitions between ideas and sentences. It successfully juxtaposes topics.

7. A composition is *well developed* when it elaborates and explains main ideas thoroughly.

8. A *consistently* written composition has a unity of content and form, mood, style, and ideas throughout.

9. A *focused* composition presents one thesis with sufficient elaboration related to that thesis.

10. An essay is *tightly organized* when it has a well-ordered, logical, cohesive, coherent sequence of paragraphs reflecting the writer's clear, unified vision of the relationships between ideas presented. The writer doesn't digress.

11. A *clearly* written composition is comprehensible, not obscure.

12. A *detailed* treatment of the topic contains many specific examples, each of which is elaborated.

13. An *informative* composition reports many facts about and/or aspects of the topic; it usually gives new information to the reader.

14. In a *penetrating* essay, the writer reveals good perception and sensitive ability to explore complex ideas in-depth. The writer often points out several sides to an issue.

15. The writer has been *precise* when he or she defines ideas and terms sharply.

16. An essay contains a *critical* treatment of the subject if the writer has exercised judgment to evaluate good and bad aspects of the topic.

17. A composition written in an *honest* manner is unpretentious and matter-of-fact in its treatment of the subject. It expresses true and sincere feelings.

18. In a *humorous* essay, the writer succeeds in being witty or in taking a novel approach to the topic.

19. A *personal* composition reveals the writer's impressions, experiences, opinions, and feelings.

20. A composition written in a *sophisticated* manner displays the writer's awareness of complex social and cultural realities.

21. A *fluidly* written essay is graceful, flowing, and articulate.

22. In a *formally* written composition, the writer avoids colloquial language and maintains distance from the reader by not being too personal, social, or chatty.

23. An essay is *figurative* if it contains metaphors and images that convey ideas in a colorful way.

24. A composition written in a *lively* way is stimulating and vivacious. It shows the writer's interest in the topic.

25. The language of an essay is *poetic* if it is similar to that used in poetry without seeming artificial or grandiloquent.

26. The essay is *subtle* if the writer suggests ideas or feelings rather than telling them in a literal manner.

27. A composition has adequate *variety* if it doesn't strike the reader as monotonous and avoids too much repetition of words, ideas, and/or sentence structures.

Of course, these definitions do not tell the full story. Sometimes, for example, an instructor might use a word like "penetrating" to refer to content or to a general impression of you as a writer. Some of these adjectives apply to some kinds of academic writing more than to others. In Table 7.1 we have classified these terms according to whether they apply to specific kinds of writing and according to whether the instructor refers to the content of the composition (what is said), its form (how it is said), or its effect (how the instructor feels about the content or style).

Take the paper you are currently working on and determine which category it seems to fit in most clearly. Then make a checklist out of the adjectives attached to that category. Turn this into questions like "Is this

TABLE 7.1 COMMON TERMS USED TO JUDGE
DIFFERENT KINDS OF WRITING

PURPOSE FOR WRITING	TYPICAL WRITING TASKS	TERMS FOR JUDGING CONTENT	TERMS FOR JUDGING FORM	TERMS FOR JUDGING THE EFFECT
WRITING TO REMEMBER	Copy Note Resumé Summary Outline	Focused Complete	Connected Developed Consistent Focused Tightly organized	Serious
WRITING TO EXPRESS MYSELF	Personal story Response journal Personal essay Portrayal Diary	Critical Personal Sophisticated		
WRITING TO INFORM OTHERS	Narrative report Description Expository composition Lab report Directions	Clear Detailed Informative Penetrating Precise Original Accurate	Detailed Precise Tightly organized Focused Developed Connected	Penetrating Serious Effective
WRITING TO CONVINCE OTHERS	Letter of application Statement of opinion Argumentative essay Editorial	Original Penetrating Subtle	Effective Consistent Tightly organized Focused	Appealing Original Clear Convincing
WRITING TO MAKE SOMETHING BEAUTIFUL	Story Poem Play	Subtle Concise Original	Fluid Formal Figurative Poetic Varied	Lively Appealing Honest Humorous

paper clear?" "Is it detailed?" As you and one of your fellow students go over each other's paper with these questions, your answers help the other make the final decision about the draft and what still needs to be fixed.

Another approach, besides questions, is to use a table that simulates the decisions an instructor might make. Let us suppose you are writing an argumentative essay; the checklist might look like Table 7.2:

TABLE 7.2 SCORESHEET FOR AN ARGUMENTATIVE COMPOSITION

QUALITY	HIGH OR LOW IN QUALITY (5–1)	COMMENTS
Original		
Penetrating		
Subtle		
Effective		
Consistent		
Tightly organized		
Focused		
Appealing		
Clear		
Convincing		

When you read each other's comments, this chart can help you understand the general emphasis of the comments and, more specifically, it can help you clarify your questions to the readers. You might ask something like, "When you said the paper was not original, did you mean that the content was too familiar or that the whole thing struck you as trite?" If you get the answer to that question, maybe you will have some information with which to make the next version better.

Another way to use this chart is to adapt to the way your instructors balance content, form, and effect in their judgments of your writing and that of other students. We have found that many instructors will focus on each of the following, with some weighting to one or more of the four:

- Content
- Form or organization
- Effect or style
- Mechanics, usage, spelling, and format

This is the grading approach we recommend in the instructor's manual for this book, and we recommend that instructors balance the four fairly evenly over the duration of the course. At certain times, however, they may emphasize one over the other.

A Set of Checklists. We have found it useful to develop a set of checklists for editing our writing; many publishers do the same thing. (You didn't think we'd have a chapter without one, did you?) The first checklist is a good one to have in mind as you read over the draft you like to see if there is one more revision you need to make. Look over Checklist 7.1 and select the items that you think are important. As you go through the list, think in terms of one particular reader or a general sort of reader that you are trying to reach.

CHECKLIST 7.1 QUALITY CONTROL QUESTIONS*

- Will readers (my reader) realize from what I have written that this is an important point?

- Will readers (my reader) be interested in this?

- Will readers (my reader) believe this?

- Will readers (my reader) understand what I am trying to say here?

- Will this convince my readers (my reader)?

- Does this sound right/good?

- Could I say this much better?

- Am I introducing irrelevant points here?

- Does this detail support my point?

- Is this sentence well connected with the previous one?

- Does this idea fit here? Is its place in the second (third . . .) paragraph, before/after the place where I talk about . . .?

- Do these facts lead anywhere? Should I put in a generalization?

- Can this conclusion logically be drawn from what I have written? Have I forgotten to say that . . . ?

- Do I need to remind my reader of my thesis here?

- Is this word appropriate in this kind of paper?

- Is this too impersonal or had I better say what I think?

Or What I Need to Keep in Mind While Checking My Text as I Write or Between Drafts

- Is this too personal/subjective, or had I better stick to the "facts" and to what others (the "experts") have said about this?

- Is this too wordy? Is it boring even to me?

- Do I need to expand this point?

- Can I even read what it says here? If so, I had better erase this and write it more clearly?

Editing

Once you have made sure that you have the content you want and in the order you want, you are ready to go ahead with the final editing. We said something about editing in the last chapter. It is the stage where you check the details of your paper. You are checking with the reader in mind, making sure that the reader stays interested and understands what you are writing. A part of this is checking the spelling and punctuation, but we want to concentrate on some other kinds of checking as well. Checklist 7.2 is a good way of following up the questions in Checklist 7.1. It presents an action plan for editing.

CHECKLIST 7.2 WHAT I NEED TO DO AND NOT DO TO MY TEXT*

- I will not change this.
- I had better give an example.
- I had better leave this out. It does not tell anything new.
- I had better cross out this sentence and rewrite it entirely.
- I had better add here the idea that . . .
- I had better change the wording here.
- I had better start a new paragraph here.
- I had better write more. This is much too short.
- I had better give reasons for my opinion here.

*Or If It Ain't Broke, Don't Fix It Just Because They Want Me to Edit

One kind of checking that we recommend is to go through the paper to make sure that you have made absolutely clear the way in which you want the reader to follow your thoughts. Use the guides to grammar and function in the last chapter to help you make sure you are clear.

Editing, the final step in preparing a paper for publication, often involves word-level concerns exclusively. Because many revision decisions add or subtract words, move them around, or change the context, you will find it necessary to go over the paper one last time. Mechanics and usage changes at the sentence level can affect the spelling of words as well. You can use mechanical aids during this last editing, but the best way to do the editing is to *read the paper aloud.* This forces you to slow down and hear what you are writing; it also forces you to attend to each word. Doing this with an audience, or being the audience when someone else reads your paper, is particularly advantageous.

Formatting and Using Graphics

Probably your instructors have special rules about formatting writing assignments. Some like double-spacing; others ask for page numbers at the top; some like the paper folded in half the long way. Some may want footnotes and references at the end of the paper; others may want them at the bottom of each page. You should be sure to check with each instructor to find out if he or she has a "style manual." That is a way of heading off having to say later, "But I didn't know what you wanted."

Below are some general aspects of format that are useful to know and follow.

- **Use only one type font in a paper.** Choose one you like and stay with it, but make sure it is readable.

- **Use boldface for main headings;** *use italics for sub-headings.* Also use *italics* or underlining for titles of books and for words that you want to emphasize.

- **Put an extra line of space between paragraphs** so that the paragraph is clearly signaled.

- **Leave a wide enough margin on all sides.** Usually make the margin 1" to $1^1/4$" on each side and an inch at the top or bottom. Some people like two inches at the bottom.

- If you are writing the paper with a pen, **use lined paper** (wide lines are usually best) and leave a good margin.

- Be sure to **number the pages.**

- If you use a table like some of the ones in Chapter 4, **label the table.** If there is more than one table, number each one consecutively. Then you can refer to each table by number.

- **Label charts or illustrations.** If there are more than one, label the them as *"Figure 1," "Figure 2,"* etc. Again, these can be referred to in the text by number. You may set the figure at any point in the page, depending on what you think is attractive. But you should generally avoid breaking up a paragraph with a figure. See Figures 7.1–7.6 for sample page layouts. The patterned boxes represent illustrations or exhibits that amplify the text.

FIGURE 7.1   **FIGURE 7.2**

Figure 7.1 emphasizes the illustration, since the eye usually goes to the top of the page first. In Figure 7.2, the illustration serves to follow the text and be somewhat subordinate.

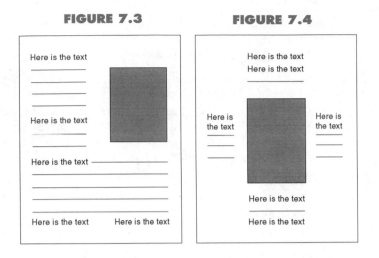

FIGURE 7.3   **FIGURE 7.4**

In Figure 7.3, the text begins to "wrap around" the picture and make itself dominate the page. In Figure 7.4, the layout is balanced and symmetrical, but it is probably hard to read since the eye does not know whether to see the picture as an interruption to the text or the text as a series of captions. It might be good for an advertisement, but not for a paper.

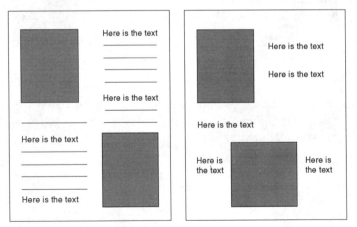

FIGURE 7.5   **FIGURE 7.6**

In Figure 7.5, the two illustrations balance the text and the result is a fairly clean view, although some would prefer to have the two illustrations on top of each other. In Figure 7.6, the layout is unbalanced, which can be pleasing to the eye, but at the same time, it is difficult to follow the text, particularly that at the bottom which can get lost. Some of these are clearly more crowded than others.

Printing and copying. Once you have the format set and you are happy with the paper you have written, PRINT IT. We suggest you print the paper on good white bond paper, not erasable or corrasable bond which can smear the ink. Make sure you print or duplicate an extra copy so that you have one for your records.

Incorporating Process Notes

As we mentioned briefly in Chapter 1, process notes or a process memorandum can be an important part of your portfolio. You will probably be asked to include some sort of self-evaluation in your portfolio. You should keep a record of your writing projects, perhaps keeping each one in a file folder where you can write a log on the inside cover to show what you did when. If you are working on a computer, you can keep an index file of drafts and copies, as well as a log file where you write down what you did each day.

In these note files it would be good to record the following: (a) how much time you spent on each part of the project; (b) a brief note on what you did; and (c) any other comment that might be useful.

The note file might look like this:

DATE	TIME	ACTIVITY	COMMENT
Oct. 5	2 hrs.	Wrote first draft of short story paper.	Need to find more examples of minor characters.
Oct. 7	45 min.	Looked up examples in Hawthorne, Poe.	These can fit in 3d and 4th pars.
Oct. 7	20 min.	Shared draft and examples with Tina and Godfrey.	Ready to add them, G says get a sharper conclusion

Once you have set up the file, it is easy to keep up as it only takes a minute at the end of the period to record what you did. You can make a separate file for each paper or keep a running diary. Either one then has the evidence you will need to explain what you did and what you learned in the course of the semester or year. When you finish a paper or a project, one of the last steps should be to go over the file and write a process memorandum in which you show where you went for information and ideas, how you planned and drafted the project, how you worked with others in planning, drafting, and revising, and any final steps and decisions you made in preparing the final version. With these sorts of notes available, a self-study or a writer's autobiography is fairly easy to write.

Having these notes can also help you keep going at a steady pace rather than trying to rush everything at the end.

Nearly Done

Now that you have chosen the draft, done the editing, gone through the formatting, and printed out the paper, you are nearly ready to turn it in. But there is one last step, a final checklist (Checklist 7.3) to use to make absolutely, positively, definitely sure you are ready to let your child go out into the cruel world to be read and graded.

CHECKLIST 7.3 A FINAL CHECKLIST*

- Did I put my name on the page?
- Did I leave enough of a margin?
- Did I spell the instructor's name right?
- Did I get someone to check the paper for typos?
- Is everything legible?
- Are all the references there?
- Are the pages numbered?
- Is it stapled or paper-clipped?
- Did I keep a copy for myself?
- Did I do my author's notes?

OK? Now I can hand it in.

*Or It Ain't Over Till It's Over

Chapter Summary

To finish each paper, you select your best draft, edit, create a format, and print (and copy, if necessary). The evaluation language in the chapter is there to help you to make these decisions, and also to make your case in a grade proposal. The final checklist is for that last look.

Once again, the computer is your friend when it comes to last-minute revisions or editing changes. In minutes you can have a revised, repaged, reprinted text.

8 Putting It All Together

Do You Know:

- Which of 10 different organizations is best for your portfolio?
- How to make final decisions about selecting pieces to include?
- How to write a self-statement and grade proposal?
- How your computer will allow you to select an effective format?

Looking Ahead

You started making a portfolio plan in the first chapter of this book. Now it's time to complete it. You'll see that putting together your portfolio presents the same problems as completing one assignment: getting started, staying with it, and getting finished.

You'll also see that, as you get ready to present yourself through your portfolio, you have many decisions to make. And these may be harder than earlier ones. These are final. This chapter includes questions to help you decide about selection, order, and presentation. You'll also see how to write a grade proposal about your work.

We began this book by asking you to look across all of your writing in and out of formal courses to see what a comprehensive picture of you as a student writer might look like. The purpose was to help you consider your various writing tasks and the way in which you work as a writer so as to assemble a portfolio. In this chapter, we will help you through the process of preparing your writing portfolio so that you may present it to a jury of students, instructors, or other people such as potential employers or admissions officers at a college, who might want to find out about you and make decisions about you.

The key word here is *"present."* You will present yourself, but not in person—and you can't present everything, and you don't have a chance to say, "Oh, but I forgot to tell you . . ." Suppose you are completing an application that says, "tell three stories about yourself that will help us to understand you." Three and only three.

Which three? In what order? The selection and organization of these stories, from the thousand that can be told and the million ways of organizing those thousand, will determine what the readers will understand about what you are like.

Putting together your portfolio presents you with the same problems.

What to select?

How to present it?

Reviewing Your Material

As we mentioned at the beginning of this book, your writing portfolio should be a comprehensive picture of you as a writer. A good writer is articulate, fluent, flexible, and able to work independently and collaboratively. We asked you to take stock of your opportunities to write, to survey your various courses to see what chances to write you had.

To help you take stock of all the writing you do, we suggested you use a checklist or planning sheet like the one shown in Chapter 1 (see Table 1.1 on p. 16.) Now is the time to take out that planning sheet and review it with all the papers in your working portfolio. As you filled out this form, some of the questions we suggested you ask were like the ones in Checklist 8.1, which go into greater detail now that you have done the work.

CHECKLIST 8.1 REVIEW QUESTIONS FOR THE WORKING PORTFOLIO

How did each of these tasks show me as an articulate writer?

- What did it tell about my handling of content? Did it involve research, coming up with my own ideas, making sharp comparisons and contrasts, or taking a new look at old material?

- What did it tell about my handling of structure and organization? Did it show that I was able to use a complicated organization and yet keep the reader following me? Were the transitions and connections sharp?

- What did it say about my handling of the language? How well did it show I knew the conventions of grammar, spelling, and punctuation? Did it show my distinctive style? Did it show how I was able to adapt my ideas to the audience?

How did each of these tasks or group of tasks show me as a fluent writer?

- How did this task show how I handled time? Were some decisions done under pressure? Did some show how I was able to make revisions? Which ones best show my range?

- How easy was it to write this? Which one presented a tough problem that I was able to solve?

- How often did I have to write pieces like this? For which ones have I a lot of examples? Which is the best sample?

- In how many different courses or situations did I write pieces like this? Can I show fluency by showing the various situations?

How did each of these pieces show me as a flexible writer?

- How was this different from other tasks in the kinds of demands it placed on me as a writer? Did I have to come up with original ideas? Did I have to come up with my own way of organizing it?

- How was it different from other tasks in the purpose or function of writing? Am I really getting a good variety of examples?

- How did it differ from other tasks in the sort of audience for whom it was intended? Was it for the teacher only? For others in the class? For strangers? For myself? Have I achieved a good variation in audiences and situations?

How did each of these tasks show me as an independent person or a team member?

- Did I work entirely on my own? How much did I have to go back to the instructor or someone else for feedback and advice? If so, how did this show in the way I worked on this piece of writing? What do I need to say about my independence?

> • Did I work with others? If so, what role did I play? How did my influence show? Was I supported by the others, or did I support them? Will the reader be able to see that we really created a unified piece of writing?

If you did not fill Table 1.1 out earlier or did not keep it up throughout the course, you can still use it to make a survey of all your assignments. Use the questions to help you sort through the various pieces. Even if your instructor has prescribed the kinds of writing that need to be in your portfolio, you will still have to make choices. In doing so you want to be sure that you show range and depth, all of those things we have been discussing in the rest of the book. Looking at your work with these questions in mind will help you determine how far toward those goals you have gone.

Above all, you want to present your best writing. You want to pick those pieces that show you at your best—and you want to arrange them so that the whole portfolio shows you at your best. At the same time, you need to be honest with yourself. Is it all right to include some pieces that are your personal best even though they didn't get the highest grade? In your portfolio it is your judgment that counts.

What about Drafts?

Some of the pieces that you wrote may exist in a variety of forms from the first notes to the finished essay. Why might you want to include these? Some instructors will insist on including a full set of drafts for at least one major assignment. It can be useful to show how you thought about and worked yourself through a project. It can show something of what you learned as you drafted the composition, shared your draft with others, got feedback, and made the changes that produced the final copy. If you decide to include a succession like this, you should be sure to include a discussion of what you learned along the way. The drafts themselves won't tell somebody the story of you as a working writer. You have to write your own version.

The Process Memo. Using your drafts and keeping tabs on them as we suggested in the previous chapter are good preparation for the process memorandum. What a judge or a reader wants to know is how you went about the particular task you have chosen. The memo need not be too long, but it should include something about how you came upon the topic and the particular approach you took, the impact of the feedback on your thinking about the composition and the feedback, a discussion of why you made the changes you did (Were you thinking of the audience? Did you change your mind? Did you find some new information or arguments to support your own?), and whether you are pleased with the results.

EXAMPLE 8.1 PROCESS MEMO

When the first-quarter marking period was coming to an end, I had to write a grade proposal. This piece was probably one of the hardest ones that I've had to write. I never really wrote about myself in the form of an evaluation-like format. I thought it over many times in my head trying to come up with a plan. I finally decided to just start writing.

I opened the piece by telling what I was going to attempt to do and how. I stated general topics I was going to relate to. I introduced to the reader what the whole piece was going to be about. I then took my ideas of turning things in on time and expanded them. I told of how I was always on time with my assignments and that I worked hard and long on each assignment, doing the work to the best of my ability. I then decided that the goals I set should be talked about. I told how I worked with my plan towards my goals and that I achieved them. I showed how I had improved and, most importantly, what I had learned from that. I then said that during my plan I learned something that was not expected. I told of how I learned it and how it helps me in my writing.

Next I figured that I would show a little about how I have taken things that I have learned in English to other classes. I described what it was that I learned in English class and then I explained how I have been able to take it to my other classes specifically and have it help me. The next to last thing I did was that I stated that for my final reason that the piece I have written shows my improvement and shows a lot of what I have learned and what it has done for me. The last part of my piece was my closing. I wanted it to be like somewhat of an introduction but to have somewhat of a summary of what my grade should be and why and that is what it is.

When I looked at this piece I knew that I had to persuade the reader to see my viewpoint. My grade for the first quarter was depending on this paper. If I didn't persuade the teacher into seeing my points and how I deserve the grade I proposed then I would end up with a grade that I didn't want. My whole goal of the paper was to get my grade to be what I proposed. I was trying to achieve this by persuading the reader, the teacher, to see my point of view and give the grade.

The idea of the grade proposal came from the teacher. The teacher assigned us to write a grade proposal to propose a grade for ourselves for the first quarter. I viewed the piece as probably the most important piece I've written so far. I just started writing ideas as to how I could persuade the teacher and how I could get my grade. When I started, I wrote first the body of my piece with all my evidence to support my grade I proposed. Next I did my ending to go along with the piece. I then went back to the beginning and wrote my introduction, which I felt was quite good because it really let the reader know what he or she should know about this paper.

My major points of decision were what supporting evidence I should use to help persuade for my grade. I had to have good strong supporting evidence that was solid and could not fall apart under pressure. I really don't feel I had any alternatives to this piece of work. I decided on what to keep and what to throw out by choosing the things I really learned from and using them. When I started this I had no idea how to go about it so I wrote a page of notes as to what I could use. Then I wrote a draft, looked it over, and then revised it into its final form. The reader that gave me a response was the teacher. He read it and he gave me a 93—a point higher than I had asked for. Once I got going the paper went well and it was very effective because I got my grade.

—Chad Bowerman

What about Collaborative Projects?

There are probably a number of writing projects that you were involved in where you were not the only writer. You and some of your classmates will probably each want to submit the project. That is perfectly all right. It is not cheating if everyone knows you worked together. But you do have to put everyone's name on it. And, most important, you each have to spell out your contribution to the joint project. The best way to do this is to share with the group the statements about each person's contribution. That way, everyone knows what the others are saying and nobody runs the risk of being accused of doing what they didn't or being what they weren't. Being honest and open is the name of the game.

The example that follows is a collaborative memorandum written by three students who worked together on a project. Notice how the memo focuses on the group contribution.

EXAMPLE 8.2 COLLABORATIVE MEMO

The Last Word: Reflections on the Collaborative Portfolio Process

It is a good feeling to produce a piece of work which you are proud to own. It is an even better feeling to have produced such work in a collaborative effort with others. The collaborative process is time-consuming. It requires commitment on the part of all group members, and the maintenance of a good communication network. However, it is a great learning experience as ideas are discussed, resources are exchanged, and questions are raised and investigated. The act of collaborative writing, which we were able to accomplish, is equally as stimulating, and thanks to the invention of notebook computers, one which can be carried on no matter where a group meets. We wholeheartedly recommend this style of work, and are grateful to _____ for providing both the opportunity and the encouragement.

What the Total Writing Package Should Look Like

Portfolios can take many shapes and forms. In whatever form you choose, the physical requirements are consistent: They should be attractive and easy to go through, comprehensive, and persuasive.

A portfolio should be as attractive as a book or album that you buy in a store. There should be a cover, a table of contents, and an easy way for the reader or viewer to go through the whole thing without spilling it all on the floor or getting it mixed up.

Work out with your instructor whether the portfolio should contain a fresh copy of each piece that you wrote for class so that everything looks its best, or whether it should simply contain the last version that you handed in. In the latter case, an observer or judge can see any comments and grades you received on the work at the time.

You should also agree on how big the final portfolio should be and on any other limitations of format. Your instructor will probably expect that all the portfolios have some common attributes such as type of binding or cover, colored paper, or labeling guidelines for joint projects or mixed-media products. It is best to know the ground rules on presentation before you hand in your portfolio, rather than after the grade has been handed out.

Make sure that you know who is going to be looking at your portfolio. It is also important to know what decisions about you and your writing will be made on the basis of the portfolio:

- How will grades be assigned?
- Will you graduate?
- Will you win the contest?
- Will you get the job?

We mention this with reference to getting permission to copy a poem or an artwork, which would be necessary if your portfolio were going to a larger public. But it is also important for you to know whether the portfolio will be judged by students or instructors whom you know, other students or faculty, parents, or a larger or different audience. In part it is simply nice if you know who will be looking at it. More important, knowing your audience for the portfolio will help you determine how much explaining of the assignment or the context you will need to give. If you had to do a critical writing assignment on *I Know Why the Caged Bird Sings*, for example, and the only audience for the portfolio were your classmates and your instructor, you would not have to explain much about the book and the task. But if your audience included parents and instructors of other subjects, you might need to explain something about when the book was assigned, about the kind of unit you were doing, and about Maya Angelou (the author).

We will go into greater detail about introductions and explanations in the next two sections. At the point of selecting material, you need to make sure that what you are choosing represents the kinds of things you can do well and can do easily. In addition to the choices based on Table 1.1, some of the decisions you need to make in selecting the material include:

- The balance between things you wrote early and late in the year: How much do you want to show growth and change? What change can you show?

- The balance between things that were judged as good and those that were judged as needing improvement: How much do you want to show of your strengths or acknowledge your limitations and weaknesses?

- The balance between finished works and works in progress (drafts or things that didn't get finished): How much do you want to show your final accomplishments as opposed to the big ideas that never quite got off the ground?

- The balance between independent projects and team efforts: How much do you want to show your independence as opposed to your cooperative strengths?

There is no "best" answer to these questions about the balance, tone, and fullness of your self-portrait. You might discuss them with your grouping partners or with your instructor; they can help.

But the final decision of what goes into your portfolio is one person's . . . yours.

Order and Presentation

Not only do you have to decide what goes into the portfolio; you have to decide how it should be arranged. In earlier chapters we have discussed possible arrangements and organizations of your various compositions and other writings. The organization of your portfolio presents the same options and challenges. Remember that your portfolio will be read by other people. You have an audience for the whole collection as well as the audiences of the individual pieces.

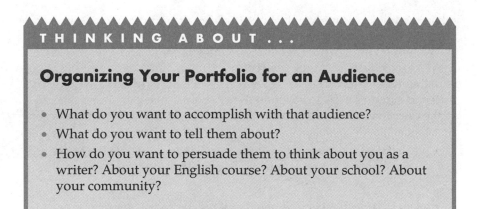

THINKING ABOUT . . .

Organizing Your Portfolio for an Audience

- What do you want to accomplish with that audience?
- What do you want to tell them about?
- How do you want to persuade them to think about you as a writer? About your English course? About your school? About your community?

Remember that no matter how large and comprehensive your portfolio, it is what your audience first sees that will make the strongest impression. No matter how many times people are told not to judge a book by its cover, they do it. In professional portfolios, it is the opening statement, the first photographs, the first 30 seconds of a 15-minute tape, or the cover that sets the impression. The rest confirms it. Your cover and opening pages will set the tone for the reading of your portfolio.

What's more, your readers will probably begin at the beginning and go to the end. Some may skip around in your portfolio the way you skip around in a magazine or an anthology. But most will go from cover to cover. If that's what you want them to do, make the order work for you.

Your readers will be looking at other portfolios as well as yours. Think about how you can make yourself memorable.

Although they will try to judge you fairly on your individual merits, remember that it's natural for them to make some comparisons. Think about how you can make yourself memorable. Also, remember that some will know you, but that to others you're just a name and a collection of stuff.

Some Organizational Strategies

Let's assume that your readers will go from front cover to back cover. Here are some possible ways to organize your portfolio:

Chronologically. Chronological organization is the most common form; it shows change and variety over time. You simply arrange the things you wrote in the order in which you did them. The weakness of this organization is that it may not result in an interesting sequence. The high point, your best paper, for example, may not have been the last one.

By genre. Sorting by genre clarifies the fluency and flexibility of your writing. You could sort your writing by such a grouping as narratives, descriptions, arguments, persuasive pieces, poems, letters, etc. You could also sort it by the functions we gave at the beginning of the book (to remember, to express, to persuade, to inform, and to please). One strength of this sort of grouping is that it makes clear the fluency and flexibility of your writing. A weakness of generic grouping is that if you have more writing in one group than in another, the arrangement will make you look lopsided as a writer.

By subject area. Arranging by subject, again a kind of classification, has the advantage of being able to show how well you can write in various fields. If you are strong in the sciences and weak in English, this can show you as a good science writer, and help soften the impression that you are not a good writer, based solely on a reading of what you have done in English. It can also be useful if you have done some praiseworthy writing outside of school. The weakness of this organization is like that of the arrangement by genre; it can show your unevenness as a writer. This can be a disadvantage in the eyes of some people, but if you are really strong in one area, that strength can outshine any area of weakness.

From practice to final project. This type of organization emphasizes you as a student of writing and as a person who takes the craft of writing seriously. You can begin with short pieces, or the ones based on various exercises, and then move on to the longer projects, the quarterly or unit projects that show your sustained effort at planning, revising, and preparing a final copy. It is a good arrangement if you can show progress and point it out in your self-statement; it has the weakness of cramming everything into the end of the portfolio.

From worst to best. Arranging from worst to best effort (or its opposite, from best to worst) can be useful to show your development as a writer and your improvement over the course of the year or semester. It uses the pattern of "I used to be . . . but now I am." Such an arrangement can be a strong argument if you have improved dramatically. But if your work has been pretty even over the course of the year, it is not a good arrangement for you. It can also be risky if you think your judges might latch onto your worst effort and have that remain their final impression.

From individual to group work. Again, this is an arrangement that can go in one of two directions. It is a good arrangement if you can show your strengths as a team member as well as those of working independently. Organizing from individual to group work is a way of showing your versatility as a writer and it is a particularly useful form of a portfolio to show to a possible employer. The problems posed by this arrangement include the fact that the material inside each group has to be organized as well, and this may be somewhat complicated.

By theme. With this form of classification of your writing over time, *you* identify writing themes; that is, the classification is made by you and not by the organization of courses or writing experts. Organizing by theme can be effective if you have dealt with one or two thematic areas in your writing across subjects and audiences. It may be that you have covered the theme of the environment in your writing in social studies and science courses as well as in English. Or perhaps a significant chunk of your writing has dealt with human relationships and the family, again across subjects.

By arranging your writing in various subjects by theme, you can show your depth and range in exploring a topic. It is a good arrangement, because it shows that you have been a serious and independent student. Its weakness is that your theme may be more apparent to you than to your readers. You should not have to explain the theme too much.

By a combination. With this arrangement of your writing portfolio, you use one or more of the preceding types of organization. You might have some writing that deals with a theme across subject areas, and you may have also written some fiction that people liked a lot. There is no reason why you couldn't include both organizations. Many other combinations of subgroupings within the portfolio are possible.

Many judges of portfolios think this is the best way to organize the whole portfolio, because you can tailor it to your own strengths. In general, we agree. But you should be sure (a) to write a good self-statement to explain these groupings and (b) to signal the groupings clearly so that readers will look at the pieces in the ways you want them to. *You are in control.* You must guide your reader through the portfolio and get the reader to see the arrangement of selections your way.

By montage or hypertext. This is an arrangement that builds up to or away from a cumulative visual effect which supports an intellectual or emotional effect. Hard to do physically, hypertext is fairly easily done on some computer programs. The selection of the materials and the arrangement (what is put next to what, how one is linked to another) have a dramatic impact. There may be a link by sequence, by amplification or expansion, by contrast, by swing in mood, by shift from action to rest. You think of the arrangement in a physical way, a visual putting together of the pieces as in a movie or a comic book. With your physical papers and projects, this arrangement can be difficult to accomplish. Some have tried using colored folders and complex boxes, but the effect is not as good as it might be unless there is some sort of display space.

With the computer technique of hypertext, however, your texts are arranged in the space on the screen of a computer and invitations to move from text space to text space are arranged by you but can also be shifted by the reader. This arrangement is a tricky one, and it is hard to do, but it can be fun. We have seen some portfolios of student writing laid out like petals on a flower or like spokes of a wheel, and others arranged in the equivalent of file drawers or the frames of a filmstrip. In Figure 8.1, the author has created a set of hypertext "spaces" illustrating various facets of her life as a writer. Each facet contains a number of compositions as well

FIGURE 8.1 A HYPERTEXT PORTFOLIO SCREEN

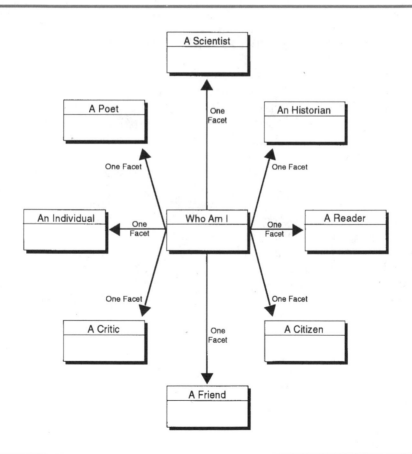

as a brief introduction, so that the reader can browse from facet to facet or explore one particular facet. In some programs, sound, visuals, and even "quick-time" moving images can be incorporated into the hypertext.

By goals. If you had three goals at the beginning of the course, you can present three arrays of work that show your achievement and progress toward attaining those goals. If you can show progress and achievement, this is a powerful way to demonstrate that you can plan and direct your own learning. You have shown that you've written your way to becoming a better writer.

Regardless of which organization you choose, it is a good idea to make some divisions of the portfolio. This will put your different kinds of writing in groups that are clearly separated from each other. You can mark the divisions physically with heavy paper, folders, dividers, or tabs. Each division might have a table of contents, or one big table of contents can appear at the beginning.

Writing the Self-Statement and Justification

As we noted earlier, the first pages of your portfolio are critical. It is best, therefore, to begin with a statement about yourself as a writer. You could have a strong short example of your writing in that opening (a poem or the beginning of an essay); you could have a comment by an instructor; or you could have an autobiographical statement. Each of these can be an effective opener. There are many others.

The self-statement should describe you as a writer and as a student, and it should set the tone for the reader. It should also help to establish the order of your portfolio and set forth your justification of that order. Generally, the self-statement begins with a one-page personal summary. It can be longer than that if you really think it is important, but one page is about enough to give your reader a first look at you. Readers like this brief introduction to where they are going to go. In the summary, you should say something about where you began as a writer, what goals you established for yourself, what you have learned in moving toward those goals, and what you think of yourself as a writer now.

EXAMPLE 8.3 SELF-STATEMENT

Introduction: The Road Map to a Successful Journey Through a Portfolio

A portfolio should be a testament of improvement and achievement. It demonstrates and documents aptitude from the commencement of the year and contrasts it with aptitude during and following the learning process in order to show growth. It is the road that shows where I have been and where I am, with mileage markers along the way as proof that I have covered the ground. As a result, you will see that I have dated the works in this portfolio. The portfolio portrays a sense of self-assessment as well. Through the duration of your journey through my portfolio, you will see those pieces that my peers and I have deemed my best work and those that demonstrate some shortcomings.

My recent areas of study have included writing essays, analyzing short stories, reacting to plays, and producing some unique and creative works. I have included pieces from a variety of these major highways in an effort to exhibit the full scope of areas explored and skills learned.

Just as I have enjoyed writing the pieces that I have included, I hope that you will take as much pleasure in reading them. Stop frequently for sightseeing excursions—you will see a wide variety of picturesque landscapes.

—Joe Osnoss

The summary in this example presents the writer as he wants to see himself. The image of the road map sets the tone of a reader's journey as well as the writer's biography. The first sentence shows us the writer's blend of pride and modesty. The general outline of contents is present so that the reader may take one of several starting points (essays, analyses, reactions, and creative works) or follow the author's order. The last paragraph creates a pleasant impression and entices the reader on to the meat of the portfolio.

The road map is but one of several metaphors portfolio makers have used. Other metaphors have included the butterfly collection, the autobiography, the museum, the portrait, the apartment house of the mind, and the market or mall. Each of these conveys an impression of who the creator is and how he or she wants readers to imagine the contents. We cannot say which one is best for you; you must choose . . . but think of the impression you are making.

Covers and Bindings

In Chapter 1 we discussed the importance of the portfolio cover and showed one example. Figure 8.2 shows another example. You may have designed a draft cover. If so, go back and review it; it is not too late to change it. Your instructor may have some specific rules about covers and bindings. Some instructors like the portfolio to be loose so that the materials can be shuffled around. Others don't mind a three-ring binder or a clip binder. Binding the materials, of course, means that readers are urged to follow your sequence. Having them loose, on the other hand, means that they can move things around. They have more control.

Since the cover is the first thing that people will see, it can help set the first impression. Covers can come in many forms and styles. They can show you as careful, creative, dedicated, original, humorous, serious, varied, thoughtful, cooperative, changing, retiring, interested, consistent, spontaneous, independent, or emotional.

This first impression can be conveyed subtly by the color of the cover. You are probably aware of the effect created by primary colors, earth tones, and shades of gray.

A photograph can form a strong impression. So can a copy of a painting or illustration.

Some writers prefer a collage. Figure 8.2 (here reproduced in black and white) is a colorful collage of the student's work, world, and self-image.

Preparing a Grade Proposal

If you have been with us through the rest of the book, you probably know what we are going to say. The message is simple and straightforward. Be honest. You know how much you have done, whether you have put in a lot of effort or have just tried to get by. You also have a sense as to whether your classmates and your instructor think you are a good writer.

Remember that the grade you receive is what you have earned by your work throughout the quarter, semester, or year. Instructors do not really give grades; they are not like Santa Claus. Grades are the tokens of your accomplishment, no one else's.

There are a number of ways to think of your grade; probably your class has discussed them. One is in relation to other people in the class. That is a form of competition, as if the class were a track meet or an art contest.

FIGURE 8.2 PORTFOLIO COVER—A COLLAGE

Another is in relation to yourself. That is a form of grading in which change and growth are the major points of focus. A third is in relation to some absolute criterion of good writing. This is competition against an external standard, and it assumes that judges have ideals in their heads as if the class were like a gymnastics competition.

Probably your program contains some elements of each of the three approaches to grading. You have been getting feedback from your instructor throughout the year, most of it probably in terms of your own growth or change. You have also set some personal goals for your writing, what you wanted to accomplish this quarter or this year. When you think about the feedback and your progress towards your personal goals, you are in a good position to estimate the grade you have earned.

Take all these things into account when you submit your grade proposal.

COMPUTERS AT WORK:

Polishing, Arranging, and Displaying

Throughout this chapter we have mentioned various uses of computers in storing and arranging your portfolio. For some courses, portfolios are stored on computer disks and the instructor or the other judges read the screen or view a projection. It is even possible that some computer writing classes are networked so that people in the class can "browse" through each other's portfolio on-line. Computer displays, therefore, depend upon the available software and the display capabilities of your operating system. If you have been keeping your portfolio items on a computer disk, the task of assembling the portfolio is not too difficult. You will have to select the files you want to include, put them in order, do the final formatting of them, and then either load them onto a disk or print them out.

Be careful about fonts. A computer offers you a vast array of type fonts and sizes. You can underline things, use boldface, capitals, and all sorts of fancy doodads. BUT DON'T. These are fine things to play with for some kinds of writing, but a readable piece of writing tends to be uniform within itself. You may make fancy title pages and dividing pages, but they should be separate from the main text. Any single piece in your portfolio should be in one font.

Choose a font and size that make the text easy to read. Most people find a 12-point type the best. They also find that a font with a serif (the little curves at the beginnings and ends of letters) is somewhat easier to read, particularly over a long period of time.

This is a sans serif type.

This is a serif type.

There are some fonts that try to look like handwriting, with the letters appearing to be connected. Generally, they are not as easy to read as those that have strong verticals and some spacing between letters.

You should be sure to check each document to make sure the items on Checklist 8.2 are set on each paper.

CHECKLIST 8.2 CHECKING ACROSS PAPERS

- Are the margins uniform across the various papers? If not, are the differences going to detract from the overall appearance?
- Are the pages numbered? Is each paper paged separately or is there continuous pagination? Which do you want given the binding you have chosen?
- Are the titles and headings correct? Do you want a single running head for all papers?
- Are the graphics where you want them? How about the size? Are tables and charts cut off from the text by page breaks?

Chapter Summary

Your portfolio is a presentation, a self-portrait. Your planning sheet and questions should help you decide the *what* and *how* of your presentation. You must consider the form the portfolio should take, key features such as fluency and flexibility, and an organizational strategy that is effective.

The self-statement and grade proposal are important parts of the portfolio. Give them as much time and care as you give the rest of your presentation.

If you are managing your portfolio on a computer, you will be able to select format, graphics, type font, and many other features from a menu of choices. When it is ready, send your portfolio off—to present yourself as a thinker and a writer.

A Final Word

The next chapter . . . isn't written here, but we're confident that it will be written—in as many styles and voices as there are people who use this book. If you know how to write, and you know how *you* write, then this won't be the last chapter in your writing career.

So there you have it, a book on writing portfolios. We have sought to bring you through the process of planning a writing portfolio, working on the writing that will go into the portfolio, and arranging the final package.

What can we say now? Not much.

You have to do most of it. No one is going to write for you unless you become so rich and famous that you can hire a ghostwriter. We hope you do, but then you can give this book to the ghostwriter, or you can use it to check her work. She may be writing the portfolio, but it will have your name on it, not hers. It will be your presentation.

APPENDIX

A Short Guide to Practical Grammar and Style

You have probably studied English grammar many times before, so we are not going to review all of the rules of grammar and usage here, nor are we going to present a whole grammatical system. Instead, we are going to present a number of grammatical points which we think will help you make your writing clearer to your reader.

One of the problems you may have had with grammar is that you weren't quite sure why you were studying it. Why did you have to name parts of speech and draw diagrams? The important question, though, is "What good is grammar and what is the grammar good for?"

What is the role of grammar? How can knowing about grammar help you? One answer is that it helps sometimes to make language the object of conscious analysis, to try to gain distance from something that is part of your daily life and activities so that you become more conscious of its possibilities and of its limitations. Grammar's relation to writing is something like physics' relation to golf; knowing helps you understand what you are doing, but it will not automatically improve your score. At its best, knowing the grammar helps you become more aware of how language works, because grammar makes something known explicitly that you often may have only felt implicitly. Our attempt to make you conscious of language cannot and need not be in any way exhaustive. Some of the basic principles are enough.

You need to be aware of the relationship between:

- Forms of language and functions of language (how language is used to perform various tasks, such as to inform people about relationships, urge them to do something, or make them feel the way you do), and that there is no one-to-one relationship: One form can have many functions and several different forms can serve a general function, such as the various ways of persuading someone to do something); and

- Forms of language and the way we organize experience (such as the verb tense system and the expression of time relations).

The basic building blocks of grammar are nouns and verbs, which is another way of saying things or ideas and what happens to them or what they do. Most sentences have a noun or a verb. Sometimes the noun is a word, like *saxophone*, but it can also be a phrase or group of words (*playing the saxophone*) or even a clause with its own verb (*That Ari played the saxophone as well as Johnny Hodges*). A verb is usually a single word like *play* but it can also be a phrase (*is about to play*). Nouns and verbs, things and happenings, do not sit alone; they can be changed, or modified, by words, phrases, or clauses. Nouns are modified by what we call adjectives; verbs are modified by what we call adverbs. The combinations of nouns and verbs with their modifiers are endless.

Getting Form to Work with Function

You can use a grammatical form to help you make your point just as well as a special word or phrase. In some cases, such as persuading or requesting functions, you can use alternative forms to nudge your reader. They are more subtle than direct forms.

Functions	Grammatical Forms
A. Persuasion	
1. Direct (the hard sell)	1. Imperatives: *Go to see **Do the Right Thing!***
2. Indirect (the soft sell)	2. Statements or questions: *Everyone should see **Do the Right Thing**. How about seeing **Do the Right Thing**? **Do the Right Thing** is playing.* (This is an indirect invitation.)

Each of these might end a review. You have a grammatical choice as to how directive you want to be.

FUNCTIONS	GRAMMATICAL FORMS
B. Request for information	
1. Direct	1. Questions/interrogative sentences: *Do you know anything about it?*
2. Indirect	2. Statements: *I wonder if anyone knows anything about it.*

In a composition, of course, you don't use this sort of request to get information but to move your reader along. To an instructor, the indirect request is less belligerent.

FUNCTIONS	GRAMMATICAL FORMS
C. Request for action	
1. Direct—conditional	1. Question: *Would you look at Table 1, please?*
2. Indirect Verbless Future Present Active Present Passive	2. Statements: *Table 1,* *Table 1 will show you . . .* *As Table 1 proves . . .* *The information in Table 1 needs to be noted carefully before . . .*

Using Verb Tenses to Straighten Things Out

Perhaps one of the most important relations between grammatical form and function is in the English verb system. Although the verb system has only a few tenses, if you consider just one—such as the simple present—you can see that it expresses many concepts and performs many functions.

SIMPLE PRESENT FORMS	CONCEPTS	FUNCTIONS
Simple present tense (in active, affirmative, declarative sentences)		
1. *It gets dark when the sun goes down.*	Permanent truth or situation	Giving information
2. *I am tired today. I have $20 in my bank account.*	Less permanent state or situation (particularly *be* and *have*)	Giving information/ indirect refusal, depending on the context of situation
3. *Marge kicks the ball to Beth.*	Quick, finished event	Giving information/ reporting
4. *Slowly the President's car approaches the bridge.*	Expected/predictable event is taking place	Giving information/ reporting
5. *We leave.*	Future event that takes place in accordance with a plan or schedule	Giving information/ overcoming objections/ refusing suggestions, etc., depending on the context

Although "voice" does not change the tense of a verb, it does affect its construction. Passive voice shifts the focus of the action. Notice that although the passive voice in English has some useful functions, you should generally avoid using it except in special cases.

PASSIVE FORMS	CONCEPTS	FUNCTIONS
1. *The window is broken.*	State/indefinite agent	Giving information when the agent is unknown or unimportant

The alternative—*Someone or something broke the window*—is awkward. Other uses of the passive follow.

PASSIVE FORMS	CONCEPTS	FUNCTIONS
2. *The experimental rats were weighed and were given the 4cc saline solution and allowed to rest for an hour. Then they were put in a maze with sixteen turns and forced to run it four times. They were then weighed a second time, allowed to rest another hour, put back in the maze, and weighed again. Five of the six lost weight.*	Sequence of events/indefinite agent	Giving information, describing, reporting/ focus on subject

When you must focus on one person or thing to illustrate a process, your sentences will flow easily if you use the passive. In the second example, who did what to the rats is unimportant, so the sentence focuses on the procedure. If only one person had performed the experiment, you could write the passage in the active voice—*I weighed the rats, injected them with 4cc.*, etc—but this way of writing shifts the focus away from the rats to the experimenter.

PASSIVE FORMS	CONCEPTS	FUNCTIONS
3. Your request has been turned down.	Event/indefinite agent	Anonymous decision-making procedure/ approval, etc., depending on context.

The form in the third example may work in some situations, but you should avoid it in academic writing. Many instructors object to the passive voice because it can lead to imprecise, irresponsible writing. You should always ask yourself whether your use of the passive voice is absolutely necessary to your meaning.

Writers use verbs, particularly the tenses of verbs, to indicate sequence in narrative and process papers. You may have heard that you should generally use consistent tenses: "Stay in the past," or "Use the present." But if you look closely at academic writing, you will find that this generalization doesn't hold up. There are both logic and a set of conventions about using verb tenses in academic writing.

Conventions in Academic Writing

We can make some generalizations on the basis of the following extracts from a research report. In looking at these extracts, you should concentrate on the tenses that the authors use to make their points. Some other stylistic features are peculiar to professional journals. You should not use them as guides for your writing.

1. When writers simply report what was done, they almost always use the simple past tense.

   METHOD

   Subjects

   The Ss[subjects] were 40 students who participated in the project in partial fulfillment of the course requirements for introductory English.

   Materials

   Presentation and test lists were constructed from a pool of 140 sentences. Six different types of sentences were included.

2. When writers report on results or cite obtained results as examples to support their generalizations, they typically use the past tense.

   Sixteen percent of the students repeated all sentences perfectly.

3. When writers state something as an asserted fact, they typically use the simple present tense.

   The results show that more students made type 2 errors than type 3 errors.

4. When writers make a generalization (something that is believed to hold for all cases and at all times), they typically use the simple present tense.

The results tend to prove that certain types of sentences are more difficult than others.

5. When writers refer to a table, figure, chart, etc., they typically use the simple present tense.

   Table 2 gives the percentages of responses in each scoring category.

   But when they cite the figures in the tables, they typically use simple past tense. (See point 2.)

6. When writers describe established use of terms, they typically use simple present tense.

   Following Smith's definition, a type 2 sentence is one without a verb.

7. When writers refer to earlier research that is assumed to be relevant to the present time or have consequences for present research, they typically use the present perfect tense combined with the present instead of the simple past, which does not have such implications.

   Smith (1990) and Wesson (1991) have both shown how useless it is to point a gun at a sentence.

   Note how this sentence implies a much stronger generalization than would a corresponding sentence which used simple past (*showed how useless it was*). The former sentence shows that the writer is much more committed to believing that what is said is a general statement of how things actually are.

8. When writers make a prediction (formulate a hypothesis that will be tested), they typically use either the simple future and "should" plus the verb. The former implies a strong assertion and the latter implies something that ought to be a logical consequence of the theory.

   If recall of sentences involves (note: simple present tense in the premise) *the reconstruction of grammar and vocabulary from an abstract list, then recall of sentences with grammatical errors and words with obscure meanings should produce particular difficulties.*

A Summary of Some Other Grammatical Forms and How They Can Help You with Certain Functions in Your Writing

Much grammar helps to indicate relationships among words—not as an abstract system, but as words that represent what you think and feel, what you want to write about. The following tabular list recaps some of the functions of grammar to indicate various conceptual relationships between such ideas and feelings, which we have discussed earlier in this book as narrative and process, cause and effect, or spatial relationships.

CONCEPTS	GRAMMATICAL FORMS
A. To indicate time relations	
1. To indicate the general order of events when things happen	1. Tense systems of the verbs: *Smith was born, Smith lives, Smith will die.*
2. To indicate the frequency of events—how often things happen	2. a) Verbs: e.g., present tense/ habitual: *I wake up at six.* b) Adverbs: *never, sometimes, often* c) Adverbial constructions: *on Tuesdays, every week, daily*
3. To indicate a specific point of time—precisely when things happen	3. a) Adverbs: *yesterday, tomorrow* b) Adverbial constructions: *at six, this evening, June 1, 1776, on the following day*
4. To indicate duration—how long things go on happening	4. a) -ing-form of the verb: *He is talking (has been talking) a long time on the phone.* b) Adverbial constructions: *I've lived here since 1980. I'll stay here for two weeks.*
B. To indicate a continued reference to something or somebody	1. a) Personal pronouns: *Churchill was in Parliament. He had two children.* b) Articles + nouns: *The man's daughter was an actress.* c) Demonstrative pronouns: this, that, these, those: *This career was a surprise.* d) Relative pronouns: *particularly to those who were snobs* e) Other demonstratives: here, there f) Temporal modifiers: now, then: *Now, no one would care.*

Concepts	Grammatical Forms
C. To indicate cause and result, a topic you will deal with frequently. You can use conjunctions that join clauses, prepositional phrases that contain cause and effect in one clause, verbs that show the relationships between clauses or sentences, indirect expressions, and, of course, a noun phrase	1. Conjunctions: a) because: *We arrived late because the weather was so bad.* b) so . . . that: *It had rained so much that the river flooded.* c) as, since: *Since it was already too late, we decided to stay at home.*
	2. Prepositional phrases: because of, on account of: *We were late because of the bad weather.* 3. Verbs: a) cause, lead to, result in, give rise to: *The bad weather caused us to be late.* b) make: *His behavior made me angry.* c) result from, be the result of: *Our failure resulted from our negligence.*
D. The roles that people, things or ideas play in the world are many, but English (unlike other languages) has only a limited number of grammatical forms or positions for nouns, pronouns, or noun phrases. These forms are called cases, and in English the three cases are the subject of a verb, the object either of a verb or a preposition, and the indirect object of a verb. Nevertheless, these three grammatical cases can indicate a variety of roles to show the writer's meaning.	
1. The actor, or who or what is doing the action in a sentence, is usually the grammatical **subject.**	*You sing very well. The rats entered the maze.*
2. The object of the action is usual-ly the grammatical **object.**	*John opened the letter.*
3. The person, thing, or idea affected by the action in sentence can be the **indirect object, object,** or the **subject.**	*I gave the money to her. John told James a dirty joke. I was struck by a falling branch. He believed he was right. [In terms of meaning, the belief affects the person.]*

Concepts	Grammatical Forms
4. The instrument or means by which an action is carried out can be the **subject** or an **adverbial.**	*The key opened the door. The burglar opened the door with a key.*
5. The location in space or time of an action can be the **subject** or an **adverbial.**	*Urbana is a windy city. April is the cruelest month. You'll find it in the drawer. We'll go on Sunday.*
6. The result of an action in a sentence can be the **object,** but in some cases it can be the **subject,** particularly if the action refers to a process.	*Mother is baking a cake. The cake is baking in the oven. [It isn't a cake until it is taken out.]*
7. The beneficiary of an action in a sentence can be the **subject** or an **indirect object.**	*I got a nice birthday present. I changed the ticket for her.*

We hope that this section on grammar has suggested to you that grammar has a very important part to play in using language. Once you realize you can use different language structures to express various functions and concepts, not only can you observe the typical relationships between functions, concepts, and forms, but also the range of all possible connections. We believe that such conscious attention to the focus of language will help you become more aware of the different possibilities you have to use language. Although later you may pay less conscious attention to grammatical matters, at first you will need to concentrate on perfecting your skills.

Other Aspects of Style

Implementing grammatical tools is one way of helping you make your point effectively, but there are other aspects of style that you should keep in mind as you prepare your writing portfolio.

Words

Clearly your writing will be known by the words you use. Some style books will tell you that you should use simple words, while others will suggest that you should use words that prove that your vocabulary is broad. We don't think there should be a flat rule about words. The English language is incredibly rich in the number and variety of words it contains. We have words for all sorts of gizmos and their parts and qualities. The vocabulary about writing itself is rich with words like *nib, chase,* and *kerning* referring to three different technologies of writing from the pen to the printing press to the computer.

There are many different words for the same general idea. A person can be *astonished, amazed, surprised,* or *taken aback* (the first literally means "hit by the thunder-stone"; the second means "to become lost"; the third means "grabbed from above"; and the fourth means "shoved backwards"). Which of the four is strongest? Which of the four would best fit the state of mind you want to portray?

Our advice is to try new words, but don't rely on a single book like a thesaurus to tell you which synonym is best for what you want to write. Accompany the thesaurus with a good dictionary, which will give you precise meanings and etymologies.

When you are writing about a technical subject, you will probably have learned a number of new words to go with the knowledge you have acquired. If the piece you are writing is for a group of people (such as your class in that subject) it is all right to use the technical terms without finding a common synonym or defining them. Be careful, however, of using that technical language when you are writing for a broader audience. This will probably be true for most of the research papers you write; you have done more research on the topic than others in the course, even your instructor. Be sure that the language is not too technical—or, if it is, that you have explained it.

Use of Metaphor and Imagery

Another way of considering words is in terms of metaphor and imagery. When should you use metaphors? Some instructors do not like metaphors; others do. To some extent, it depends upon the course you are taking. In most subjects there are a lot of metaphors which people almost don't recognize, but the experts want the writing to be as "literal" as possible. In mathematics, for example, there is talk of "fuzzy logic"; is this a metaphor? Of course it is; it is saying that logic, the way people are trained to think, is like an object that has gathered a lot of dust or fuzz so that it is no longer smooth. Why should thinking be smooth? What is the "fuzz?" The metaphor is what some people call a "dead" metaphor (that is a metaphor about metaphors), and they tend to think of it as a literal description of a kind of logic.

So, people use metaphors all the time, but what about using them consciously? Making up new ones? What about taking abstract ideas like *logic* and using other words to describe it so that people can have the sense of seeing it or hearing it? Our general advice is that in most writing, even poetry, you want the metaphor or the image to be firmly attached to the idea you are putting across and not to call attention to itself and distract the reader. If you are writing about logic, you might use metaphoric language like *fuzzy, smooth,* or *sound.* But a sentence like the following may be carrying things too far.

> *When mathematicians and computer scientists think about logic, they now see it as something that has been pushed under the sofa for too long and has gotten so many dust kittens attached to its once billiardlike surface that the original sphere is no longer visible.*

Sentence and Paragraph Length

One of the frequent pieces of advice you will hear is "Vary your sentences and paragraphs." That's a nice idea, but how do we do it and why? To our mind, the advice has to do with the question of rhythm and, particularly, visual pattern. Most writing is seen and not heard. So its appearance on the page or the screen has an effect on the reader. Although people like some order and similarity in what they see, they do not like to see a landscape that has no variation, like a row of houses that are all the same. This is also true of writing. Most people like sentences and paragraphs to have some predictability (that's where grammar comes in), but they don't like monotony.

Sentences. There is no ideal length for a sentence, although the average for most mature writers in English is about 11 words. Sentences can have as few as two words and the top number goes into the hundreds for some writers. More important than length of sentences is their pattern. Sentences have to have a noun and a verb, a subject and a predicate—*John jumped.* The subject, however, does not always have to be first and the verb second. Sometimes you can reverse the order. (*More important than length of sentences is their pattern.*)

The normal way of changing the order is to use what are called "free modifiers," adjectives or adverbs that can move around in the sentence.

> *Skipping around the room, Alyse teased John about his increasing baldness.*

> *Alyse, skipping around the room, teased John about his increasing baldness.*

> *Alyse teased John about his increasing baldness, skipping around the room as she sang.*

Moving these modifiers around can be one way of changing the length and appearance of what you write. How does it change the focus of the ideas in the sentence?

Length can also be changed by combining sentences into larger groupings.

Elvira opened her mouth.

Her two fangs glistened.

The moon shone on them.

Elvira approached Raul's neck.

Raul's neck was bare.

Raul was sleeping.

This would be pretty monotonous. There are a number of combinations that can be effective, depending on the focus. Try writing four variations: one with two sentences, one with a focus on the moon, one with a focus on Raul, and one with a focus on the two of them equally. Combining short sentences like these is what you do all the time as a writer. If you want to practice this kind of combining, there are a number of books available that let you experiment with pre-made sentences. You can also work with your own material. One way to do this is to take your entries from a reading log or journal and experiment with combining the pieces.

Paragraphs. The length of paragraphs is a similar matter to that of sentences. There is no perfect length and shape. A paragraph is a visual chunk of your writing, meant to be taken in at a single sitting. Since it is visual, a part of the determination of length may be how it looks on the page. Most people do not like to see a whole page without a break. Normally they do not like to have more than two or three breaks on a page either. At the same time a short, single sentence paragraph can be a great attention getter, but be sure it contains the part that you want to stand out.

In English used in the United States, the main point of the paragraph usually comes at or near the beginning and may be repeated at the end. In other languages, the point may be at the end or it may be repeated at various intervals. We recommend that you vary the placement of the main point somewhat, but keep it in the first three sentences of the paragraph.

Repetition and Change

How much variation should you put into your writing? We have suggested that too much of the same thing can be monotonous, but some repetition can be effective. There is a rhythm to a sentence or a group of sentences that can be used to advantage. In the eighteenth century, Edward Gibbon wrote,

The true interest of an absolute monarch generally coincides with that of his people. Their numbers, their wealth, their order, and their security are the best and only foundations of his real greatness; and were he totally devoid of virtue, prudence might supply its place and would dictate the same rule of conduct. [Decline and Fall of the Roman Empire, *New York, Modern Library, n.d. I, 106*]

The first sentence is short, and the second is long; its length is broken in half, with the first half containing a series introduced by *their*. This repetition builds up a momentum that keeps the reader going to the end of the first clause and into the second. The second part is also divided in half with the last word of the first half, *virtue* immediately followed by its alternate, *prudence*. The two are to be contrasted and then at the end of the sentence produce the same result. The pattern of these sentences can almost be plotted like the rhyme scheme of a poem. What appears to make the sentence and its idea stick in our heads is the use of repetition, just like that in Lincoln's "government of the people, by the people, and for the people." If the *their* or the *people* were not repeated ("their numbers, wealth, order, and security" or "of, by, and for the people"), the punch of the sentences would be lost.

Repetition and the building up of a rhythm are important stylistic features. You should not overdo them but use them as parts of your stylistic toolkit.

Styling a Paper

In Chapter 4, we presented this brief research paper. Let's look at it again from the perspective of language and style.

Isn't this just wonderful! I should have expected this from the start. If only they hadn't evolved into such intelligent creatures! Well, at least they all seem to think that they're so incredibly intelligent, but . . . oh, never mind. Anyway, it's happening already. And I only had them fooled for sixty thousand years. Not very long at all on a universal time scale. I always thought, or hoped, really, that it would take longer than that for them to figure this entire situation out.

You see, they didn't used to be this way. They really weren't all that bright in the beginning. They did evolve from primates, you know. It was quite simple, really. For example, death. Not a very difficult concept to grasp. One day you're quite active, next day you're stone dead. So, naturally, they began to wonder about this mysterious phenomenon, inquisitive creatures that they are. And, since their limited anatomical knowledge left them with absolutely no hope of determining the cause of this unfortunate circumstance, they made something up, supported by the theory stating "If God did not exist, it would be necessary to invent him." (Voltaire, Epitre a Auteur du Livre des Trois Imposteurs*)*

*At first, it was nature. You know, the rocks, the trees, the water. Yes, water spirits, definitely water spirits. Animism is the theory one would logically imagine to explain natural phenomena, right? But, as they ever so slowly gained in intellectual power, they began to wonder not only about what made the wind blow, or where a newborn child comes from, but things like the origin of the universe, the existence of subatomic particles, multiple time oriented realities, simple stuff like that. So, of course, water spirits just didn't cover it any more. (*The World Book, *Vol. 16)*

This is where I come in. The Supreme Being, creator of everything. End of story. Well, not quite. You see, I was able to hold their inquisitiveness in check for a while with a few neat tricks like the Inquisition. After all, if you kill all of the intellectuals in a given world, who's going to tell the rest of them that I really can't logically exist. But, the intellectuals countered with the Renaissance, and look at the result! There's no doubt about it. They're discovering the truth! (W. Durant, The Age of Faith*)*

Why is this happening? What's wrong with them? After all, I must lend them some sense of security. Anyone would feel better if he or she had their own supreme being watching over them, right? "Naught but God can satisfy the soul." right? (P. J. Baily, Festus: Heaven*) Of course I'm right, I'm supreme! But they don't seem to think so anymore, or at least not all of them. But why? After all, everything I stand for is so right for everyone, so practical. Males labor to support the females, who need not pursue an education since their main purpose is to raise their children, which they conceived as a result of procreational, and definitely not recreational, 'knowing.' And there will be several of these children since the evils of contraception, and, worse yet, abortion, are strictly not permitted. (*The Bible. *Genesis)*

Despite all of these wonderful morals I've provided for them, and the emotional support, and all of the 'knowingly' frustrated men in black, they're losing faith. And you do, of course, know what the consequences of that are, don't you. Well, "Religion without mystery ceases to be religion," as one of them so accurately stated it. (W. T. Manning, Sermon Feb. 2, 1930*) And that is definitely not good for my mental health. You see, when they no longer believe in me, I simply cease to exist.*

—Joshua Tallent

This paper is intended as a monologue and as a satire, but it is intended to be read silently, not read aloud. The speaker is talking in the present but is giving the whole scope of human history in four paragraphs, so that the tenses include both present (the comments) and the past (the events). The movement back and forth in time is well handled as is the generally ironic tone. As a document to read, however, the paragraphs are all about the same length and the effect could be heightened if the last sentence were given its own paragraph. Another point of monotony is the use of the quotes and citations at the end of the paragraphs, and the use of a single style of citation. Instead of "one of them," the writer might have put "As W. T. Manning put it in his sermon of February 2, 1930, "Religion. . . . ." There are also a few places where the words are not clear: "universal time scale," "limited anatomical knowledge," "'knowingly' frustrated men in black." In each case there might be a better or more accurate word ("eternal," "diagnostic," "mesmerizing" might be good alternatives. In terms of grammar, the sentence "And there will be several of these children since the evils of contraception, and, worse yet, abortion, are strictly not permitted" is not ungrammatical, but confusing. There is a long span between subject, *evils*, and verb, *are strictly not permitted*, which, when added to the surprise of having an evil not permitted instead of being forbidden, causes the reader to stop longer than may be useful for the irony to sink in.

Each of these is a relatively small point of style, but taken together they keep the writer from being as sharp a satirist as he would like. Each of them—the grammatical points of ambiguity, the use of tenses, the length and variety of the paragraphs, the placement of the quotations—is something that the writer or a friendly editor might notice and sharpen.

Using a checklist for revision and editing can help, but nothing helps as much as reading the paper over again with a fresh eye. You may love what you have written when you wrote it, but when you become the revisor or editor you become a reader, not the genius with a gift for words. Remember what we wrote at the beginning: That readers are likely to be bored and to misunderstand. That is the sort of reader you have to be with your own writing. Then with a fresh eye you can convince even yourself that you are really pretty good.

INDEX

A

Abstract writing, 105–106
Academic writing
  cause and effect in, 72–73
  comparison and contrast in, 73–74
  defining topic in, 66–69
  getting started in, 65–79
  organization in, 71–72
  problem solving in, 76–79
  steps in, 69–70
  verb tense in, 240–41
Active language, 186–87, 191
Adjectives, 236, 246
  to indicate time relations, 242
Adverbials, 244
Adverbs, 236, 246
  to indicate time relations, 242
Analogy, 60
Analytical writing, 85, 90–91
  organization pattern for, 91
Argumentative writing. *See also*
    Persuasive writing
  scoresheet for, 205
Art, writing assignments for, 140
Articles (*a, an, the*), 242
Assessment profile, 34
Attitude, in writing, 109–10
Audience
  defining, 31
  explanation of work for, 222–23
  needs of, in revision process, 180–81, 186–88
  organizing portfolio for, 224
  payoff, 84–85
Autobiography, 54

B

Bindings, 230
Biographical approach to formal
    writing, 162
Brainstorming, using computer for,
    79–80
Business, writing assignments for,
    141–42

C

Cases, 243
Cause and effect, 65
  grammatical forms to indicate, 243
  tracing, 72–73
Characters, sociological model in
    describing, 168–69
Charts, labeling, 209
Chronological organization, 224–25
Clarification of ideas, 183
Classification
  external and internal logic in, 85–86
  forms of, 71
Clauses, revising order of, 190–91
Collaborative memo, 221
Collaborative writing, 12, 140, 221
Comparative approach to formal
    writing, 163
Comparing and contrasting, 73–75
Compilation stage, 216
  appearance of portfolio in, 222–24
  checking across papers in, 233
  covers and bindings in, 230, 231
  fonts in, 232
  grade proposal in, 230, 232–33

Formality, determining level of, in
writing, 107–8
Formal writing, 162
biographical approaches to, 162
comparative approach to, 163
cultural approach to, 162
definitions in, 170–71
evaluative approach to, 163
formalist approach to, 162
historical approach to, 162
interpretive approach to, 163
lists in, 171
philosophical approach to, 163
plan in, 171–72
reader-response approach to, 162
Format
criteria for, 12
general aspects of, 208–9
Found objects, writing about, 62–63
Freewriting, 36–37
in research plan, 122, 124–25
Future tense, in academic writing, 241

G

Generic grouping, 225
Goal setting, in writing, 8–10, 12–13,
228
Graded papers, adapting, for new
uses, 195–96
Grade proposal, for presentation
portfolio, 230, 232
Grading system, 10–11, 201–202
Grammar, 235–44
Graphics, adding, to final draft, 208–
11
Grouping technique, 12–13

H

Halliday, Michael, 144
Health, writing assignments for, 142–
43
Hierarchy, creating, 71–72
Historical approach to formal writing,
162
Home economics, writing assign-
ments for, 141–42

Homonyms, checking spelling of, 192
Homophones, checking spelling of,
192
Hypertext program, 112, 226–28

I

Ideas
clarifying, in revision process, 183
explaining to audience, 187–88
Illustrations in amplifying text, 209–11
Imagery, 245–46
Imperatives, function of, in persuasion, 236
Indirect object, 243, 244
Informational writing, 87–90
patterns of organization in, 88
Inside/outside perspectives, 52–53
Instructor
criteria of, for evaluating portfolio, 194–95
negotiating goals with, 10
Internal logic, 86
relating to purpose, 94–96
Interpretive writing, 90–91, 163
pattern of organization in, 91
Interrogative sentences
in persuasion, 236
in requests for action, 237
in requests for information, 237

J

Justification, 228

L

Laboratory report form, 146–47
Language
and audience needs, 186–87
literal versus figurative, 106–7
writing assignments for learning,
143–44
Learning log, 34
List, establishing, 71–72
Literal language, 106–7
Literary writing, 20–21, 162–73